T0145632

HOW TO HELP
SOMEONE AFTER
A MISCARRIAGE

The mental health & wellbeing publisher

ABOUT THE AUTHOR

Clare Foster is an award-winning writer, trainer and community manager. As a writer, she develops supportive information content for a wide range of health charities and companies. She has written for the Miscarriage Association, Action on Postpartum Psychosis, Mind, Bupa, the British Lung Foundation, MindWise, BBC Radio 1 Advice, The Mix, Couple Connection, The Recovery Letters, Standard Issue, Prospect, *The Telegraph* and *The Guardian*. She blogs at clarerosefoster.co.uk and tweets @fostress. She lives in the Chew Valley, Somerset, with her husband, two sons, cats Haddock and Calculus and collie Dr Watson.

HOW TO HELP
SOMEONE AFTER
A MISCARRIAGE

A Practical Guide to Supporting Someone after a Miscarriage,
Molar or Ectopic Pregnancy

Clare Foster

TRIGGER™
The mental health & wellbeing publisher

This edition published in 2023 by Trigger Publishing
An imprint of Shaw Callaghan Ltd

UK Office
The Stanley Building
7 Pancras Square
Kings Cross
London N1C 4AG

US Office
On Point Executive Center, Inc
3030 N Rocky Point Drive W
Suite 150
Tampa, FL 33607
www.triggerhub.org

Text Copyright © 2021 Clare Foster
First published by Welbeck Balance in 2021

Clare Foster has asserted her moral right to be identified as the author of this Work
in accordance with the Copyright Designs and Patents Act 1988.

All rights reserved. No part of this publication may be reproduced, stored in
a retrieval system, or transmitted in any form or by any means, electronically,
mechanical, photocopying, recording or otherwise, without the prior permission of
the copyright owners and the publishers.

A CIP catalogue record for this book is available upon request from the British Library
ISBN: 978-1-83796-254-9
Ebook ISBN: 978-1-83796-255-6

Typeset by Lapiz Digital Services

Trigger Publishing encourages diversity and different viewpoints. However, all views,
thoughts and opinions expressed in this book are the author's own and are not
necessarily representative of us as an organization.

All material in this book is set out in good faith for general guidance and no liability
can be accepted for loss or expense incurred in following the information given. In
particular this book is not intended to replace expert medical or psychiatric advice.
It is intended for informational purposes only and for your own personal use and
guidance. It is not intended to act as a substitute for professional medical advice.
The author is not a medical practitioner nor a counsellor, and professional advice
should be sought if desired before embarking on any health-related programme.

For tiny Sprout, who lived inside me for seven short weeks and died in August 2019.

FOREWORD

Miscarriage is a sadly common experience, with an estimated one in four pregnancies ending this way. Despite this, it is mentioned only briefly in pregnancy books, so while most women and partners know that it is something that *can* happen in early pregnancy, they don't expect it to happen to them. If it does, it can be a very shocking event, both physically and emotionally.

We also don't talk about miscarriage very much. It often takes a celebrity talking about her or his experience of loss for us to get a sense of its impact. Sometimes that opens the doors for others to share their experience, but many stay silent. And if they do share, they may find that family and friends simply don't know what to say.

This book fills these gaps. It is thoughtful, helpful and inclusive. It is rooted in years of empathic enquiry and research on the topic of pregnancy loss – not as an academic exercise, but as a basis for developing and improving care, support and information for those who experience miscarriage, ectopic pregnancy, or molar pregnancy.

As with all the work that Clare has done for the Miscarriage Association, she has started by asking those at its centre for their experiences, thoughts, views and needs. Most have been women and their partners who have been though pregnancy loss, but Clare has also researched the experiences and needs of health professionals, family and friends and, most recently, employers and managers.

The pages that follow are far more than a sum of these parts. Clare highlights the wide range of feelings and reactions during and after pregnancy loss, the different impact that each experience can have on each individual and the diverse needs of those affected. Just as important, she acknowledges the difficulty of those who want to offer help, but aren't sure how to, or when. She makes it easier for them to understand and empathize, and offers practical suggestions, with knowledge and also with humility. Few writers would note, as she does:

"I'm aware that I will have selected and edited these experiences through the lens of my own understanding and experience. If I haven't represented anything like your experience or that of the person you are supporting, I'm truly sorry."

This is what makes for such a special book, for which many, many people will be grateful.

Ruth Bender Atik
National Director
The Miscarriage Association

CONTENTS

INTRODUCTION

"The strange and hardest thing about miscarriage is that it's an unacknowledged loss. Prior to it happening to me, I would have had no understanding of the pain, heartache and physical process. Only when I openly talked about my experience did I find out that nearly everyone I spoke to knew of someone who'd had a miscarriage. I know of no one who has been absent from work citing miscarriage as a reason, and the most common way of dealing with it seems to be to have an operation, take a few days or a week to heal and carry on as normal. We need to understand and respect the loss of a baby – a future – and the physical and emotional healing that needs to occur."

Amy M

If you've picked up this book, it's likely that someone you know has been through a miscarriage, ectopic pregnancy or molar pregnancy. You may be a partner or a close family member. In which case, I'm so sorry for your loss too. I want to help you navigate this difficult time, and have included information and support for you, as well as suggestions for what you can do to help. I know it can sometimes be really hard for partners to support each other, especially if their feelings about the loss are different. We'll look at this in more detail throughout the book.

You may be a friend or co-worker. The support you can offer will depend on your relationship with the person, or people, involved. But everyone can offer something – and it can make a real difference. A simple 'I'm sorry for your loss' can go a long way.

You may be understandably uncertain about how to be supportive. The range of experiences and reactions to a loss can make it hard to get it right. While many people feel grief, some find that framing their experience in terms of bereavement or baby loss doesn't make sense to them. There may be lots more people like this who don't feel the need to share or speak out at all.

You may be too worried about getting it wrong to take the risk, or think that it isn't worth saying anything unless you can 'solve' the problem. It may feel too uncomfortable to acknowledge and sit with their emotions, whatever they are.

"I didn't know much about miscarriage before my sister's experience and to be honest, I still don't know enough. I wanted to offer her support, but I was worried about

giving false hope, wrong advice, getting in the way and saying the wrong thing. I tried to give her a lot of emotional support, comfort foods and some help with housework, so she didn't have to worry about that.

The most difficult thing was making sure she knew she was allowed to show her emotions and be vulnerable, as she felt she had to put on a brave face for everyone else. She would ask for cuddles and say she just needed to talk. Other times it was clear she needed a hug or wanted to cry, but that she needed me to offer that and tell her it was OK to cry. She was worried she was being a burden."

Sarah (supporting her sister who had five miscarriages)

Sadly, I can't give you a magic wand to make everything right. I can't give you all the answers or a script that is guaranteed to help everyone. Instead, I hope this book will go some way toward helping you understand what has happened, how the person you are supporting might be feeling and what it might help to say or do. It may shock you, or make you question your own assumptions or ideas. You may find it very hard to understand some feelings or responses. That's OK. Just try to keep in mind that it's how *they* feel that is important right now. Thank you so much for being prepared to learn, for making the effort to try and help.

PERSONAL STORIES

This is not just my book to write. While I have experienced the devastation of a missed miscarriage, there are thousands of stories of loss, of endurance, of grief and pain, of relief or guilt, of acceptance or of ongoing struggle. They are often kept behind closed doors. The more we hear their voices, the better we will understand. I have included as many different experiences as I can throughout, in the person's own words where possible. Many of those who shared their experience were doing so for the first time. Some found it cathartic. Everyone said how important it was to be able to share, to tell others and help them understand.

There is not one story and one reaction, but as many different experiences as there are women and men who go through loss in pregnancy. All deserve the support that is right for them. Of course, I'm aware that I will have selected and edited these experiences through the lens of my own understanding and experience. If I haven't represented anything like your experience or that of the person you are supporting, I'm truly sorry.

I've referred to lots of useful organizations and charities through this book. You can find more information about them in Useful Resources and the Endnotes.

"Whenever I have shared my experience, without fail, someone has said 'I've had a miscarriage,' or 'My sister/ friend/wife/girlfriend has had a miscarriage.' I think normalizing it as something that is sadly common and part of many people's experience is really important. I felt very alone at the time and maybe if I knew just how common miscarriages are, I wouldn't have felt so isolated, or like we had been singled out for anything other than something that's a natural part of many people's experience of having children."

Gavin

"It's been the texts that simply ask, 'How are you doing today?' that have been most helpful. Those are the people who have walked alongside me as I've dealt with the grief. They haven't tried to fix me, and I think that's really important for people to remember. They want to make things better, and that's really understandable, but it's not possible to fix things. And looking back, the more anyone tried to 'fix' me, the more broken I felt."

Eliza

TERMS USED

This book is intended for everyone. I have used the pronouns 'she' and 'her' to refer to the person who was pregnant and has experienced the physical loss, while acknowledging some men may carry a baby.

Partners are, of course, both male and female. I have used 'they' and 'them' to refer to partners, and also when referring to the woman and her partner together (if she has one).

In general, I have used 'baby' rather than 'embryo' or 'foetus', as this is the term I most often hear used by those who have experienced loss. I understand this isn't right for everyone and explore this in more depth in the chapter on talking about miscarriage.

For ease, I have sometimes used 'miscarriage' to refer to all three types of loss.

1

ABOUT MISCARRIAGE, ECTOPIC PREGNANCY AND MOLAR PREGNANCY

If you want to offer support, it can help to know the facts. People have told me that they feel less alone just knowing someone has made the effort to find out more about what they are going through. Having said this, if you want to share information, it may be more helpful to guide them to leaflets and support organizations rather than giving them a rundown of facts and statistics. Keep in mind that everyone's experience and reaction will be different.

MISCARRIAGE

A miscarriage is the loss of a baby before a certain number of weeks in pregnancy. After this it is called a stillbirth. The number of weeks at which this cut-off falls varies around the world. In the UK it is defined as the loss of a baby before 24 weeks gestation. In Australia and the US, it is before 20 weeks. If a baby is born alive at any time, even if they only live for a short while, this is considered a live birth.

People who have what is called a 'failed transfer' of embryos in fertility treatment, or those who have a 'vanishing twin' – a second embryo that is absorbed by the woman's body very early on – may feel they would prefer their loss recognized and described as a miscarriage. Many people who lose a baby later (for example in the second trimester) feel that the word miscarriage doesn't describe their loss in the way they would like it to. The fact that we cannot agree on a worldwide definition of miscarriage emphasizes how vague and culturally determined these boundaries are. It's worth always following someone's lead in terms of the language they use.

"Many parents choose to do something to remember their baby's life. For example, they may have a private burial, their own ceremony, plant a fruit tree or make a donation in their baby's memory."

UK law requires stillbirths (after 24 weeks) to be registered, but there is currently no possibility of registering a pre-24-week loss.[1] (An expert group in England and another in Scotland is hoping to change this, so that there is an option for voluntary registration or certification.) This lack of registration can be really difficult for some parents, making them feel that the death, and therefore the life, of their baby has not been properly recognized. Many parents choose to do something to remember their baby's life. For example, they may have a private burial, their own ceremony or something else, such as planting a fruit tree or making a donation in their baby's memory.

TYPES OF MISCARRIAGE

There are different kinds of miscarriage. Very early miscarriages *may* be physically (although not emotionally) more like an extremely heavy and painful period, although they can last a long time, hurt a lot more (some women say it's like having contractions) and involve the loss of many more blood clots. Even at eight or nine weeks pregnant, a woman may pass a tiny recognizable embryo. Later miscarriages usually involve going through labour in order to give birth to the body of a tiny baby.

If a miscarriage starts to happen naturally, the first signs may be blood loss. There may also be pain and cramping. Miscarriages are usually confirmed with a scan. Some women end up going to the Emergency Department (ED) because they are not sure where else to go. The ED is not the best place for someone experiencing a miscarriage. Although the person may be desperate for help, and hope that earlier intervention will lead to a better outcome, ED staff may not have the resources to treat it as urgent so there may be a long wait, while experiencing heavy bleeding. Sadly, in many cases, there is no intervention that will prevent a miscarriage from happening.

Sometimes a scan will be inconclusive and women are told they may have to wait a week or more to have another scan. This is to give time for a very early pregnancy to grow. For people who are desperate to know if their baby is OK, this wait can feel almost intolerable.

Sometimes a baby dies, but the levels of pregnancy hormone do not drop immediately. This means the woman will experience signs and symptoms of pregnancy, perhaps for weeks. This is called a missed or silent miscarriage and the parents may only find out their baby has died at a routine scan.

EMMA'S EXPERIENCE

A Loss at 16 Weeks and Another at Six Weeks

The sonographer was silent while she took some measurements. I could see my baby lying still, with no familiar white heartbeat ticking away. After what felt like a lifetime, the sonographer simply said, 'I think you know what I'm going to say ... I'm so sorry.'

I was told I would have to have an induction and vaginal delivery as, at 16 weeks pregnant, this was the safest option. I had to take a tablet to effectively stop my pregnancy, go home and return two days later to be fully induced, and go through labour and birth. The thought of being at home for two days with a dead baby inside me filled me with utter horror.

Two days later we returned to the maternity hospital, entering the bereavement unit through a back door. I was induced via pessary and within ten hours, after a painful labour, our son was delivered at 11.33pm. My husband and I were alone in the room at the time and despite the tragedy it felt like a special and intimate moment. Our son was red, shiny, gunky-looking, but utterly perfect in our eyes. He looked like a serious soul and had his right hand resting on his hip and head, upturned slightly in a warrior pose.

We spent hours with him, parenting him even though he was gone. I was completely inconsolable when I handed him back to the care of the midwife. I'm not sure how my legs carried me out of the building and away from him forever.

It's listed as a 'miscarriage'. However, I view it as anything but. He was nestled away inside me safely. He just died. I had to be induced, labour and deliver him. It wasn't quite stillbirth, but in my eyes it was not a miscarriage.

The second loss was so different. A scan at six weeks confirmed that we had lost the pregnancy the day after the bleeding started. I knew already the pregnancy was over as I had passed a huge clot and could see the egg sac within it.

> *It wasn't a physically painful loss – it just looked like a normal period after that clot passed. We were discharged with nothing more than a leaflet and apologies. Completely different and almost brushed aside. Thank goodness I was already under the care of a counsellor I could trust.*

WHY DO MISCARRIAGES HAPPEN?

We don't know a lot about why miscarriages happen, particularly in individual cases. In the small number of cases where a cause can be found, investigations and treatment may make a huge difference, but most people don't ever find out why. This can be hard and it means it could keep happening. But it also means there is no reason why the next pregnancy (if there is one) should not be healthy.

Research has suggested there are a number of possible causes: a genetic problem with the number of chromosomes in the embryo, a problem with the development of the placenta, a blood-clotting condition, a problem with the cervix, the shape of the uterus or an infection.[2] A lot more research is needed.

What is really important to remember is that it is very, very unlikely to have been caused by anything the pregnant woman has (or has not) done. This doesn't stop anyone feeling guilty or wondering if they should have done things differently.

The Miscarriage Association has some good information and reassurance in their leaflet *Why Me?* [3]

> *"I felt guilty. I went over everything that had happened between my first and second scans to try to determine what caused the miscarriage. I blamed work, stress, crying, the flu jab, the shopping bag I carried home. The doctors had said it was likely to be a chromosomal abnormality, but there was no definitive answer, which made it easier to torment myself."*
>
> Claire

TREATMENT AFTER A MISCARRIAGE

Sometimes, the baby and pregnancy tissue will be expelled naturally from the womb. This is called a complete miscarriage. Extra physical treatment may not be needed, although many people may benefit from further psychological support.

In an incomplete miscarriage, pregnancy tissue is left behind. When this happens, or when the miscarriage is only discovered at a scan, additional treatment may be needed. Many hospitals will start by suggesting natural, or expectant management, which means going home and waiting for the miscarriage to start naturally. Another option is medical management – using medication to speed up the process – which may happen in hospital or at home.

Both these options are very likely to involve severe cramping and blood loss, including heavy clots. The cramping is sometimes described as like strong period cramps, but it's more like the contractions of labour. It could take a long time and a recognizable embryo or foetus, possibly still in the pregnancy sac, may be passed. Some people prefer to hold and see their baby, whereas others find it traumatic.

The last option is surgery to remove the baby and pregnancy tissue, done under general or local anaesthetic. The procedure used to be called ERPC, which stands for Evacuation of Retained Products of Conception, but understandably, a lot of people found this terminology upsetting and it shouldn't be used any more. It is now called surgical management of miscarriage (SMM) or manual vacuum aspiration (MVA).

AMY M'S EXPERIENCE

Six Weeks of Haemorrhaging After Expectant Management for a Missed Miscarriage

We turned up for our 12-week scan, excited to see our new baby for the first time. The excitement in the room turned to shock when the sonographer said that she couldn't find a heartbeat. We slunk downstairs to the NHS Early Pregnancy Unit (EPU) for another scan and to hear our options. Sitting in a waiting room with happy, smiling pregnant people was unbearable and I passed the time shaking and crying.

Within a few minutes I had to choose between an operation, an induced natural miscarriage or a natural miscarriage at home. The latter was recommended as the safest and best choice. Feeling totally overwhelmed and always preferring the natural approach, I took the last option and was astonished to be discharged from the NHS without any healthcare support. I was told there would be pain (so to buy my own paracetamol) and that if my haemorrhaging got bad I should go to the Emergency Department.

The next ten days were easily the worst I have ever had in my life. My body still thought it was pregnant, whilst I knew my baby was dead. I knew that at any time I could start miscarrying and I was terrified as to what exactly would happen as no one had actually prepared me.

My midwife friend explained to me that the pain I had been told to expect was actually labour. I would need to dilate to 4–5cm to release the baby and the placenta from my womb. I would deliver a baby and this might be a shock for me to see. Ten days after the scan, the cramps started, then turned into contractions – I suddenly felt an urge to go to the toilet. Whilst sitting there, I delivered a tiny but perfect baby. He fitted into the palm of my hand. I could see eyes, fingers and everything. Blood and clots poured *out of me. Night became morning and I fainted in the bathroom, waking up in a pile of gore. I spent the next six weeks flat out in bed recovering and waiting for it to stop. I still had placental residue and membranes in my womb months later.*

My physical recovery was long due to the amount of blood I lost, but this was nothing compared to the emotional processing. In pregnancy your hormone levels are tens of thousands of times higher than normal. It takes time for these to come down and rebalance. Your mood is up and down like a yo-yo. You also have to start coming to terms with the loss of your baby, the pregnancy and the future that you had invested in.

ECTOPIC PREGNANCY

An ectopic pregnancy happens when the fertilized egg embeds somewhere other than the uterus, most often in a fallopian tube (sometimes called a tubal pregnancy), but it can sometimes be in other places within (or outside) the reproductive system[4].

In the early weeks, the pregnancy can appear to be progressing as normal. As the baby grows, it can cause pain, internal and external bleeding and rupture (tear) the walls of the fallopian tube. A ruptured fallopian tube can be life-threatening.

The only way to treat an ectopic pregnancy is to end the pregnancy and remove the baby, using medication or surgery. Often, the pregnancy and the fallopian tube are both removed.[5] Sadly, it isn't possible to move the baby to the uterus.

An ectopic pregnancy can be a lot to cope with. She may have been in a lot of pain, or had her fallopian tube removed and have to come to terms with the fact she nearly lost her life as well as a fallopian tube and her pregnancy.

She may be worried about her fertility, but in most cases, even if one fallopian tube has been removed, fertility will only be slightly affected. The other fallopian tube can pick up eggs from either ovary. The Ectopic Pregnancy Trust has some good information on trying to conceive after an ectopic pregnancy.[6]

Like miscarriage, it isn't clear what causes ectopic pregnancies. There are some known risk factors including an infection in the uterus, fallopian tubes or ovaries, endometriosis, smoking cigarettes, being over 35 or having had abdominal surgery.[7] But many women who have an ectopic pregnancy have none of these risk factors – and many women with these risk factors still have successful pregnancies.

Don't lose sight of the fact that an ectopic pregnancy is still the loss of a baby. Other people may focus on the risk to the woman's life or the surgery, while she may be more upset by the end of the pregnancy. Saying 'I'm so sorry for your loss' is still likely to be appropriate (see page 92).

ECTOPIC PREGNANCY EXPERIENCE

An Ectopic Pregnancy after Seven Years of Fertility Treatment

After seven years of fertility treatment, we finally fell pregnant. We spent ten days in the most blissful bubble. We had a delicious secret and couldn't wait for our scan at the fertility clinic.

The scan was an internal one as it was estimated that our baby was only seven or eight weeks. The sonographer was moving the wand around, pushing and prodding for what felt like hours. Then she questioned me about whether I was absolutely sure that I was pregnant.

She couldn't find a heartbeat. After more prodding she told us that 'the foetus is ectopic'. It was in my fallopian tube. I didn't know what ectopic meant, but recognized that it being in my fallopian tube wasn't good.

I felt devastated that what we had wanted for so many years had turned into this situation. The most glorious bubble of excitement had been burst and all of our plans had to start from scratch again.

A doctor told us I needed emergency surgery to remove the foetus and potentially my fallopian tube. The foetus was still 'heart beating' – it was important to remove it ASAP so that it didn't grow any further and rupture my tube.

> When I woke up I was groggy and desperate to see my husband. When we got back to my room it was dark. My husband was sitting there in pitch darkness – no one had called him to tell him that I was OK and he had feared the worst. Selfishly, it was the first time that I considered how all this had affected him.
>
> The following week I had lots of trips to and from the NHS Early Pregnancy Unit to measure hormone levels and check the wounds. My hormones showed that my body still thought I was pregnant and we had to monitor this in case I had retained tissue that would need to be removed. We were told that we would need IVF to conceive in the future as I only ever ovulated from my right tube and that was the one that they had removed.

MOLAR PREGNANCY

Molar pregnancy[8] (sometimes called *hydatidiform mole* or *trophoblastic disease*) is when a fertilized egg with the wrong number of chromosomes implants in the womb. This is either because two sperm fertilize the egg instead of one so there is too much genetic material (a 'partial mole') or there is no genetic material inside the egg at all (a 'complete mole'). When this egg implants, the cells that should become the placenta grow far too quickly and take over the uterus. The levels of pregnancy hormones can be very high, so women with molar pregnancies may have strong pregnancy symptoms, including sickness.

In a complete mole, no baby grows at all – instead, the cells that would have become the placenta grow to fill the uterus. Some women don't think of this as a baby, but may still mourn the pregnancy they thought they had. Others will feel very much as if they did have a baby, and lost it. In a partial mole, a foetus with a heartbeat may be seen on a scan but sadly, in most cases, this will end in miscarriage.

Occasionally these cells can bury deep into the lining of the uterus. This is called an 'invasive mole' and it can be cancerous if it is not treated. Although this cancer has a cure rate of nearly 100 per cent, it is still likely to be very scary.

Sometimes, the fact the pregnancy was molar is not discovered until a check is done on the remains of the baby or placenta after a miscarriage. If someone has been through natural or medical management of a miscarriage at home, they are usually advised to do a pregnancy test a few weeks later. If this comes back positive, it may mean the pregnancy was molar and hormone levels are still high as a result.

After a molar pregnancy the woman needs regular checks of urine or blood to make sure the level of the pregnancy hormone hCG has fallen. If the hCG level rises, the woman may have to have further treatment. In some cases, she may need chemotherapy. The hCG level sometimes drops quite fast, but for some it can take weeks or months of slow drops and plateaus. This waiting and uncertainty can be exhausting, scary and frustrating.

Even after the hCG level comes down, the woman is advised to wait until after her follow-up monitoring to try to conceive again, in case she needs additional treatment. Follow-up monitoring can last for a further six months after the first test showing 'normal' hCG levels, which can create a feeling of being in limbo and make it difficult to move on. The small percentage of women who have chemotherapy are advised to wait a year after the end of the course before trying to conceive.

Like other forms of pregnancy loss, we don't know a lot about what causes a molar pregnancy. Age, ethnicity and previous molar pregnancies can all be risk factors. The key is that it isn't anything the woman has done.

Someone who has been through, or is going through, a molar pregnancy and its aftermath may need a lot of support. It is rarer than the other forms of loss we have discussed and many people, including health professionals, may not have heard of it. The woman may be confused and anxious and people around her may not be able to reassure her. Some people may think that there never was a pregnancy there in the first place – just a lot of abnormal cells – which may make it harder for them to understand or imagine how the woman might be feeling.

The woman may need help finding others who have been through something similar (see Useful Resources) and be supported to ask questions and advocate for themselves as they come to terms with what has happened and the ongoing tests they must endure.

RECURRENT OR MULTIPLE LOSSES

Some people have many miscarriages, one after another for years. They may feel stuck in an exhausting cycle of trying to conceive, enduring the waiting and anxiety that comes with early pregnancy, and the devastation of another loss. They may also live with the fear that they will never have a successful pregnancy (or another one if this is not their first child).

"People who suffer multiple losses need the same, or even more, support and care each time."

People do not get used to pregnancy loss. Most find each new loss harder and harder to cope with. Their situation may feel like an ongoing bereavement that does not get easier. They may spend months and years of their lives in discomfort, anxiety or pain as they go through trying to conceive, possibly fertility treatment, early pregnancy, loss and then waiting for their cycle to return – repeatedly. It can feel like their life is on hold. It's hard to make plans or focus on other things. There is an uncertainty that is always present, even in a pregnancy that lasts into the second or third trimester. It's never an easy yes or no, but it's also very hard to say 'no more', to change course so dramatically. Who is to say what is worth it or not – and how does anyone know, themselves? Many women and their partners endure, and endure silently for a long time. Some manage to have a successful pregnancy eventually, but sadly some do not ever have a live child.

People who suffer multiple losses need the same, or even more, support and care each time. It can be a real strain on couples – one or both of them may find it helpful to have someone else to talk to.

2

THE PHYSICAL AND EMOTIONAL IMPACT

In this chapter I want to help you understand how confusing and complicated the time after a loss can be. Not everyone will experience all of these effects, but most people will experience at least some.

PHYSICAL EFFECTS

The physical impact of a pregnancy loss can make everything harder to cope with. Even if the woman feels OK emotionally, or even relieved that the pregnancy is over, she may need support to cope with the physical symptoms.

She is likely to be very tired. If she has had surgery, she will need some time to recover, which might include bed rest.

It may take some time for her hormones to readjust. She may experience severe mood swings and low mood, with particularly bad premenstrual tension (PMT) before her next period (usually after about 4–6 weeks). Her cycle may take some time to return to a regular pattern.

The woman is likely to bleed for a while, and this may be on and off. Some women bleed for three months or more, which can be exhausting and a constant reminder that things are not back to normal. She may feel uncomfortable using sanitary pads, particularly if she is used to using tampons or a period cup (not advised after a loss due to risk of infection). She may experience cramps or other pain. If these get worse (more painful or longer lasting), she should seek medical advice.

> "I miscarried at just over nine weeks, and having contractions so early on was a shock, as was the amount of tissue passed once things got going that first night. I bled for 12 more days, but I had things planned so I tried to pretend it wasn't happening. I tried to act like my former self. I enjoyed the pretending and periods of forgetting – until the next time I had to rush to the toilet. Being faced with more blood was repeatedly surprising and upsetting. As was feeling it leave at any given moment. I am not used to wearing sanitary towels and am hyperaware of them, especially when they overfill."
>
> Esther

Some women want to return to their pre-pregnancy body as quickly as they can, as looking pregnant or carrying more weight is a difficult reminder of what they have lost. Others may want to hold on to the look and feel of being pregnant for longer.

Women who experience a later loss may have sore breasts and leak milk, which can be really upsetting. A supportive bra, painkillers and breast pads can help reduce the physical discomfort. A nurse or midwife should be able to advise on how to reduce the production of milk, if that is wanted. Some women choose to pump and donate to human milk banks (to nurture premature or ill babies in hospital, or for mothers who can't nurse their babies). Some may like to bury some milk with their baby's body.

"Everyone reacts differently to a pregnancy loss, so be led by the person you are supporting."

EMOTIONAL EFFECTS

"We went through different emotions at different times and that sometimes meant we weren't on the same wavelength. In the early stages of pregnancy, it was difficult to fully appreciate what was happening – there is no 'sign' of it, no belly, Amy had no morning sickness, she just described *'flutterings' and things like that. So, as a man, I just had an idea of what was happening. I think that's why I always felt like I was playing 'catch up' with her and my own emotions when we had the miscarriages. I remember a lot of numbness in the first few days after a miscarriage, it not immediately sinking in. The upset came later. I remember anger too and I definitely remember jealousy of others and guilt over that. Miscarriages come with a lot of shame and guilt."*

Keyan

It's worth emphasizing that everyone reacts differently to a pregnancy loss, so be led by the person you are supporting. We shouldn't diminish grief, but neither should we imply someone 'should' be feeling something they are not. This is important within a relationship, as well as among family and friends. Dismissing or minimizing any emotion can cause shame or encourage people to internalize difficult feelings.

I've tried to represent all the emotions and feelings about loss that I've heard or been told about. I'm very aware that failing to represent everyone can make those who are left out feel even more isolated. I'm so sorry if this is you. There is perhaps a greater emphasis on the ones that seem more common, that people speak of more. The most important thing to remember is that whatever the person you are helping is feeling is real for them, and the best support you can offer is to recognize this.

It's also worth remembering that feelings can change. Someone who feels OK at first may struggle at a later date.

A DIFFERENT KIND OF LOSS

For many people miscarriage, ectopic pregnancy or molar pregnancy is a different kind of bereavement. It is the loss of a person that will now never be.

However briefly, there was a possible future, a whole human life ahead. Pregnancy tests are much more sensitive now, meaning many people are aware of their pregnancy earlier. The apps and websites that many couples download as soon as they get a positive result are illustrated with tiny babies and rarely mention the likelihood of loss. Many people can't help but start to imagine the future, to bond with their potential baby and do all they can to nurture it.

Miscarriage is the loss of the hopes, dreams and plans that grow with a positive pregnancy test, but may have been planted years ago. These are plans that go to the very core of a person's life and their family.

"The physical effect of the loss, exhaustion, tiredness and hormonal changes can exacerbate emotions and make them harder to cope with."

When everything suddenly changes, it can take a while for those expectations to catch up. For many people there is a fresh wave of grief every time they are reminded of everything that would have been, but now never will be. This may be partly why the stage of pregnancy at which the loss happens does not equate to the 'level' of grief. There are other factors too – for example, the length of time it took to conceive, the number of losses, family history and how the expectant parents were treated by medical staff.

The physical effect of the loss, exhaustion, tiredness and hormonal changes can exacerbate these emotions and make them harder to cope with.

Some people may be able to put the loss behind them reasonably quickly. Some may find that they experience grief later on, perhaps at anniversaries, on Mother's Day or if they get pregnant again. Others grieve their loss continuously for a long time.

"It felt like I was in a fog. I felt ashamed and embarrassed, like I'd failed. The first miscarriage seemed to have a big impact for a long time. The second, third and fourth had no less of an impact in their own right, but I think the cumulative impact of it all has been huge. Every time you have a miscarriage it chips away part of your soul, and you can only go through it so many times until you lose yourself completely. We are now expecting every pregnancy to end

in miscarriage. But there's also defiance, a determination to love the next baby for as long as they're in this world. One of the things that helped me emotionally was knowing that each baby had only known love."

Eliza

TRYING TO UNDERSTAND

If you've lost a family member or friend, you know how bereavement feels to you. If you haven't, you may be able to imagine what it would be like and the support you would want. You are likely to have seen bereavement on TV, in films and in your wider circle of friends.

> "You may have to accept that you will never fully understand, but you can certainly try to get a sense of how the person you are supporting might be feeling."

It's much harder to imagine how someone might feel after a miscarriage. There are no life experiences or shared memories to grieve, which may be why people experience miscarriage in different ways and some partners or family members find they have diverse feelings about the loss.

This can make it harder to offer support, or even to bring it up at all. Miscarriage is rarely talked about or represented in the media. You may have to accept that you will never fully understand, but you can certainly try to get a sense of how the person you are supporting might be feeling.

> "She was initially very angry and confused, but I said right from the off that whatever she was feeling was a valid response and she should allow herself to feel each emotion. I think this helped her as her family (unintentionally) had been quite unsure of how to handle her grief, and therefore either didn't want to talk about it, or had the 'Well at least you've got your son', or 'You're still young, you can always try again!' approach, which I knew from my own experience was not hugely helpful."
>
> Leah (who had a pregnancy loss herself and supported a number of friends)

COMPLICATED EMOTIONS

Even if the pregnancy was unwanted, a loss can be suddenly and unexpectedly devastating. Some people may feel relief, but also sadness. Feelings can be complicated and may be confused further by the sense that they are the 'wrong' feelings to have. Many medical professionals are wonderfully kind and caring, but some are more dismissive. Workplaces can fail to offer appropriate support and this can make people question their reactions too. If their boss says, wrongly, that they are not entitled to leave (see page 48), they may feel they should be up to working, even if they most definitely are not.

Some people think that having a child or children already should lessen the blow of the miscarriage. It may do, but often it doesn't. Questioning emotions can make things feel even more muddled. Part of your role is accepting anything the person you are supporting is feeling, and helping them to accept it too. Grief and sadness are not the only emotions they may have (if they are feeling these at all). They may feel angry – at themselves, at fate, at the hospital, at other people with babies – or just have an incoherent sense of rage.

"I was unprepared for how the grief would affect me. I have never felt such intense anger before in my life. I couldn't understand it. The rage. It was the grief."
Claire H

Those who have experienced a pregnancy loss often say they feel lonely and isolated, jealous of other people and, for a while, unable to cope with daily life. Some women feel embarrassed or stupid – as if they should have realized their baby had died inside them.

"I had a huge feeling of shame that I'd told people and that they must have thought I was an idiot for believing it was going to be fine. I was also ashamed of being off work because I didn't really have any symptoms and I felt I should just keep going until the miscarriage started. And I felt like I was making it up – I hadn't even actually had a miscarriage, as such. I was just an idiot who hadn't realized her baby had died six weeks earlier. I was also clearly faulty for not being able to make this baby properly."
Ruth

A loss can also bring with it feelings of failure. The woman may feel she has let down her partner or family. They may be worried about conceiving in the future. This can be exacerbated if she has had a fallopian tube removed (see page 11), if it took her a long time to conceive or if the baby was conceived through fertility treatment.

"Miscarriage is a horrible experience, no matter what the circumstances. I think miscarriage from fertility treatment is particularly hard as sometimes the woman or couple does not have the financial means to 'go again'. It's not that simple. With fertility treatment, to actually get pregnant is a massive ordeal, and often women and couples are pretty exhausted mentally and physically by

the time they get to that point so a miscarriage is going
to hit them very hard."
Claire H

There can be a period of being in limbo, waiting for the menstrual cycle to adjust and ovulation to return. After a molar pregnancy (see page 13), couples are advised to wait at least six to eight months before trying to conceive.

Some people are desperate for a child, but feel scared to conceive again and unable to cope with the anxiety a new pregnancy will bring (see Chapter 8). If they don't know why they miscarried (and most people don't), there may be a horrible feeling of not being able to control whether it happens again. An anxious mind can imagine endless worst-case scenarios.

> "The feelings and thoughts involved
> may be a constant background noise in
> their lives – hard to see past, but almost
> impossible to live with."

Conception, pregnancy, loss and birth can become charged with additional emotions and uncertainties. These can surface unexpectedly and may take some unpicking.

Even a long time after the loss, there may be a fresh wave of grief, anger or jealousy at reminders, or when seeing babies or pregnancy announcements.

For those who have experienced multiple losses, it may never be far from their minds. They may be remembering past losses, trying to conceive, worrying about time running out, feeling anxious about a new pregnancy, taking a break from trying, or coming to terms with childlessness. The feelings and thoughts involved may be a constant background noise in their lives – hard to see past, but almost impossible to live with.

"I'm constantly steeling myself against something I know will hurt me, and trying to heal myself after it has. Mother's Day. Father's Day. Every pregnancy announcement, birth announcement and baby bump I see on the street goes through me. Most conversations I have with people about children are tinged with sadness and longing. I hope it won't always be this way – that we'll either have success or stop trying, and gradually, somehow, start to move on."
Claire

Finally, it's important to mention those people who don't feel as if their losses were something to mourn. They are less likely to speak about them to anyone or to seek support. You may never know they happened, but we should be aware of the whole range of possible responses.

"I've a had a few early losses and a vanishing twin. I don't believe I lost babies, I don't identify with #babyloss, I haven't talked about it with anyone except my husband (and don't want to) and I didn't experience any grief or trauma. I felt disappointed and a bit wistful about what might have been, but that's all."

Katie

EFFECTS ON A PARTNER

Don't forget that partners need support too. If you are a partner yourself, Chapter 4 is specifically for you.

"We [partners] are also battered by the waves of emotion that come with loss, but we are meant to be the rock, steadfast and unflinching – the strong silent type. As she was pushed from one clinic to the other, jabbed with needles and given internal examinations, I could only take control of the practicalities. A month after our return I phoned work to tell them I was sick. I didn't tell them that I had burst into tears the previous night and felt like I wanted to constantly sleep. Even now there are days I feel

despondent and I can't help but feel I am a sadder person
than I was two years ago."
Keyan

Partners may feel the same, or similar, emotions as the woman who experiences the physical loss, but may show them in different ways. They may feel they have to be strong or find they get less support. Keeping feelings to themselves can mean they don't manage to accept and process them, which may cause problems further down the line. Female partners may find they are left out by health professionals or are not accepted as co-parents. This can be really hurtful.

In some cases, partners may grieve differently or move on more quickly. This doesn't mean they wouldn't find it helpful to talk to someone, or at least have their feelings, and their loss, acknowledged.

"I remember the hospital appointment a few days later,
the sense of dread and the waiting around. I remember
basically being a spare part – definitely nobody offered
me support, but I wouldn't have expected any as I
wasn't being operated on. When my wife came out of
surgery a nurse told me to look after her as she would
be emotional. She was upset; I don't remember feeling
anything except concern for her. It was definitely a low

week or so, but very quickly it was a sad memory rather than anything more."
Gavin

MISCARRIAGE AND MENTAL HEALTH PROBLEMS

"Once the adrenaline and anxiety of the last couple of months receded, mourning took its place. This time, I didn't wait around and saw my doctor for antidepressants. I'd had enough of trying to navigate the grief of infertility, IVF failure and pregnancy loss using only my internal resources. They were depleted, and I felt traumatized by the past few weeks. I needed additional, chemical support. I had counselling. It was appreciated, but not as useful this time."
Claire

For some people, the way they feel after their loss or losses will be an expected and natural part of grieving. For others, their loss (or what happens afterwards) may cause or exacerbate mental health problems. The line between the two may feel blurred.

We don't know exactly what causes mental health problems, but research shows links between miscarriage, ectopic pregnancy and Post-Traumatic Stress Disorder (PTSD), depression and anxiety. It may be the trauma of the loss itself – the shock, blood, fear and the experience of giving birth to something that may be recognizable as a tiny developing baby, potentially without warning.[9]

It may be what happens afterwards. How the person is treated can make a big difference to how they cope. As can how they respond to this treatment and what they feel about how they are coping. Women may feel it is their fault, or question their emotions and feelings relating to the loss. They may be physically or emotionally isolated, thinking about the loss and worrying about the future. Changing hormones can cause or exacerbate low mood and anxiety. It may become more difficult to manage an existing mental health problem. They may worry that existing treatment (for example, medication) has played a role in their loss. If they have used unhealthy coping mechanisms in the past – for example drugs, self-harm, alcohol or have had a difficult relationship with food – they may use these to help them cope.

Some people have, or receive, a diagnosis. Others don't have a diagnosis, but experience difficult symptoms (for example panic attacks, intrusive thoughts, flashbacks or insomnia) for a long time. The UK charity Mind has some useful information on specific diagnoses and symptoms, as well as more information about trauma.[10]

"All the time, I was getting graphic memories of the losses arriving completely unbidden, but found myself unable to stop vividly recalling every detail. At the time, it felt like something I must be doing to myself – why was my brain forcing me to relive all this pain? Why was I letting myself think through the whole damn thing for hours in bed, including the worst bits – especially the worst bits? I felt stupid and ashamed and guilty and pathetic, like I was purposefully wallowing. I now know I was likely one of the many women who experience symptoms of PTSD following pregnancy loss."

Amy

There is even less research into a partner's experiences of mental health problems after a pregnancy loss. We do know that in some cases, partners internalize difficult feelings, which can lead to persistent grief in the long-term.[11] In the sections about speaking to a doctor and seeking counselling, I have used 'them' and 'they' to refer to the person you are supporting. This is in recognition of that fact it may be a woman, her partner or both who need additional help.

Supporting someone who is struggling with their mental health can be emotionally and physically exhausting. You may find it difficult, frustrating and upsetting. It's important that you look after yourself too (see Chapter 9). Part of this might involve thinking about what you can do and accepting what you can't change or do alone.

It's not up to you to decide if someone has a mental health problem, but you can be there for them and help them get any additional support they need. Most people will talk to someone close to them about how they are feeling before they seek professional help.

SPEAKING TO A DOCTOR ABOUT MENTAL HEALTH AND PREGNANCY LOSS

Local doctors are often the first port of call for people who are looking for extra help. Some are wonderful at helping people with both mental health problems and pregnancy loss. Sadly, others are less so. Both can be difficult and sensitive subjects and not all doctors have the necessary training or understanding to say the right thing and offer the best help. Some of these suggestions may help you to get the support the person needs from their local healthcare system.

- Suggest they ask to see a doctor they feel comfortable with – and ask for a double appointment if needed.
- Writing things down before the appointment can help them remember what to say – especially if they have to undergo telephone triage before a face-to-face appointment, something which has become much more

common due to the Covid-19 pandemic. Some people find it helpful to give these notes to their doctor in the appointment too.

- Offer to attend the appointment with them.
- If the doctor isn't very helpful, encourage the person you are supporting to try to see a different one. It's common to feel disheartened and reluctant to continue to seek help if the first person you see is unhelpful or hurtful, but there are doctors who are very understanding and supportive.

THERAPY AFTER A MISCARRIAGE

"In retrospect, I really wish I'd sought some therapy at the time, just to process it all. I carried my depression for such a long time and it had a huge impact on my daughter's early months and years. I couldn't tell friends and family what a fraud I felt, or how ashamed. If I'd been able to put it to rest at the time, then the next couple of years could have been so much easier. Three years later I eventually had therapy and although it covered a range of issues, my anger, shame and sadness about the miscarriage and my husband's response were still a huge part of it."

Ruth

Some people find it really helpful to talk to a therapist/counsellor after a miscarriage. A good therapist can give women and/or their partner space to work through difficult feelings, and strategies to cope.

Therapy can sometimes be accessed through the hospital where they were treated, through a charity, place of study, doctor or workplace. Some private therapists specialize in, or at least understand, pregnancy loss. Having said that, it's worth remembering that a therapist without specific experience of pregnancy loss may still be experienced in working with some of the feelings involved – low mood or anxiety, for example. Most therapists will offer an initial consultation for free. If things don't feel right, it's worth looking for someone else. A good relationship with the therapist is often more important than the type of therapy.

"A good therapist can give women and/ or their partner space to work through difficult feelings, and strategies to cope."

The person you are supporting may feel daunted by the idea of speaking to a therapist for the first time, especially if they are feeling low and anxious. They may want to get some additional help, but at the same time find the idea of talking to a stranger very scary. Therapy can sometimes make things feel harder before they improve. They may just not feel ready to talk yet.

Accessing therapy has to be their decision and feel right for them. You can't force it, but you can offer them support on the day – perhaps even going with them to an appointment. Help them think about what they want to say and anything they want to ask beforehand. Be there afterwards with a hug, or to talk things through. If you can't be there physically, send a message or give them a call.

The Miscarriage Association has a really useful filmed discussion with a specialist therapist about therapy after a miscarriage.[12]

MEDICATION FOR MENTAL HEALTH

The person you are supporting may worry that medication she took during pregnancy caused or contributed to her loss. If she is offered medication after a loss, she may worry it could make it more likely she will miscarry again. Partners may also be prescribed medication – but this section is focused on people who may need to decide whether to take medication alongside pregnancy. I have used 'her' to refer to these people.

There is very little research into medication and its impact on pregnancy. It's understandably almost impossible to get ethical approval for controlled experiments on pregnant women and their babies. That which exists is based on observation rather than experiment. Updated NICE guidelines[13] in the UK say that doctors should discuss the benefits of medication and the consequences of *not* having treatment for the woman and any future baby as well as any possible harms associated with treatment, or with stopping medication abruptly. These benefits and harms can vary considerably depending on the type of medication involved.

Whether the woman starts or continues to take medication is entirely her decision. A doctor can help by providing adequate information and advice. You can help by talking through her options, doing some research for her and giving her different perspectives to think about. Here are a few things for you, and her, to consider:

- Some medications are considered safer than others. Very few are specifically not recommended. Coming off any medication should be done slowly and with support from a doctor. A doctor may also be able to suggest a safer alternative, if there is one.
- One of the most common medications prescribed for mental health problems is a Selective Serotonin Reuptake Inhibitor (SSRI) antidepressant. The UK's NHS guidelines say that there is currently no evidence that common SSRIs are associated with miscarriage, preterm birth or

low birth rate.[14] Overall, it is thought that the risks of not treating depression and anxiety outweigh the risks of antidepressants to both mother and baby. Maternal depression can be associated with increased substance misuse and preterm births. Women with depression who stop taking antidepressants just before or during pregnancy are at greater risk of relapsing before or after birth.

- The woman may want to try other options first – for example, therapy (see page 116). Her doctor should be able to suggest or refer her to other sources of support.

- High levels of stress and anxiety *may* make it harder to conceive – the research isn't conclusive.[15]

- Lots of people trying to make this kind of decision find it helpful to read about others' experiences and talk to people who have been through something similar. Exploring others' experiences of conception, pregnancy and breastfeeding whilst taking a particular drug may help the person you are supporting decide what she feels most comfortable doing.

- It's worth being aware of the difference between absolute and relative risk. You may hear that something doubles the risk of something else. These statements can be scary, but you need to know what the risk was to begin with. If the risk was absolutely tiny, doubling it is still a very tiny level of risk.

TALKING TO A DOCTOR ABOUT MEDICATION

These are some questions it might be helpful to think about/ ask a doctor when thinking about taking any medication, not just those to treat mental health problems.

- What are the potential benefits of this medication in the short- and long-term?
- What are the possible consequences of not taking this medication in the short- and long-term?
- What are the harms associated with this treatment?
- What are the risks of any of these harms happening anyway?
- What might happen if the treatment is changed or stopped?

ROSE'S EXPERIENCE

Taking Sertraline through Two Successful Pregnancies and a Miscarriage

I have been on an SSRI antidepressant since I was 17. At 32 a doctor advised me to try to come off them before trying to conceive. Even tapering off incredibly slowly over three months was too difficult. I felt incredibly anxious, something that could only be managed by excessive exercise and restricting my food. I lost a lot of weight, couldn't sleep and my periods stopped. I started getting intrusive suicidal images. Eventually I saw a different doctor who told me he would not recommend coming of SSRIs before trying to conceive, as it adds unnecessary stress and anxiety. I went back on 50mg Sertraline, recovered slowly and eventually conceived my son.

I stayed on Sertraline throughout my pregnancy. My son was born healthy and has no problems. My doctor and I increased my dose to 100mg after nine months as I struggled with insomnia and anxiety.

Two years later, we started trying to conceive again. Unlike the first time, I got pregnant immediately. Twelve long sick weeks later we were told at our dating scan that the embryo had stopped growing at seven weeks. It was devastating. I opted for surgical management and struggled to manage grief combined with mood swings as my hormones settled over the next months. I wanted something to blame. I started to try to reduce the Sertraline.

Very quickly, the sense of dread, the panic and the insomnia returned to an unbearable degree. I returned to 100mg every day. I tried to accept that I needed this medication. It was the baseline from which we would do our best to build a family, however we could.

> *A further long seven months later and we conceived our second son – still healthy in there at 34 weeks. My relationship with my medication has been complicated, but I've accepted I need it – for my sake but also for my husband and children. They need me to be able to function and parent effectively and, for whatever reason, Sertraline is part of what I need in order to do that.*

SUICIDE AND HARM

Suicidal feelings can be a symptom of a mental health problem, a side-effect of medication or a result of a traumatic life event (a stressful, frightening or upsetting experience – for example, losing a baby). The charity Samaritans say that most people who feel suicidal do not want to die – they do not want to live the life they have. Some people have a plan; others experience distressing but abstract thoughts about ending their life or what that might look like.

It's OK to ask the person you are supporting if they are thinking about suicide. Research shows that asking someone directly about suicide is not likely to 'put the idea in their head'.[16] Instead it gives them permission to tell you how they feel. It's important to stay calm (even if you feel upset about what they are telling you), listen, ask direct open questions and take them seriously.

If you think someone is in danger, the quickest way to get help is to call emergency services, remove anything the person could use to harm themselves and stay with them until help comes.

The UK charity Mind has some good information online – search 'Supporting someone who feels suicidal'.[17] It's important to look after yourself too (see Chapter 9).

3

WHAT ELSE COULD BE GOING ON?

"Life doesn't stop because you're having fertility problems or miscarriages. As well as trying to grieve our miscarriages, I was also dealing with a restructure at work, serious family illness, a new dog, studying part-time, anxiety, insomnia, fertility treatment, the mental gymnastics of constantly counting cycles and relationship difficulties ... on top of a full-time job, trying to maintain other relationships and putting on a brave face for the world. It was exhausting, but I didn't feel I was able to talk about how tired I was because I couldn't cope with the comments of 'Wait until you have children – then you'll feel tired."

Eliza

Miscarriage, ectopic and molar pregnancies, and their aftermath, can affect many aspects of daily life. Understanding what else could be going on will help you offer more thoughtful support.

ONGOING APPOINTMENTS

There may be ongoing appointments or tests, which can make it harder to move on, if that's what the person you are supporting wants to do. It may be tiring or difficult for her to travel to hospitals or clinics, so she may appreciate the offer of a lift. If appointments are in work hours, she may be reluctant to tell work why, which may make it harder to get the time off she needs.

WORK

Not all employers are understanding or supportive of an employee's needs after a pregnancy loss. Discrimination faced by women of childbearing age means the person you are supporting may not feel able to tell her place of work the real reason for her absences.

Leave that is related to pregnancy should be recorded separately and must not be used against a woman in any way.[18] Leave after a miscarriage (if confirmed by a doctor) counts as pregnancy-related. This means women should be allowed to take as much time off as they need to recover without it affecting their record. Not all employers know this – and of course, to take advantage, women need to be prepared to talk to their employer about their loss in the first place. It may be worth the person you are supporting finding out if her employers have a miscarriage policy.

Partners are not legally entitled to any leave, although may be given compassionate or bereavement leave (paid or unpaid). Many partners have to return to work before they are ready, or before the person who experienced the physical loss is ready to be left.

"Many people are forced to return to work before they are ready. They may find it hard to put on a brave face – if you work with them, the offer of a coffee and a chat may help remind them that people are thinking of them and give them the opportunity to talk if they want to."

And of course, even if the leave is recorded correctly, unless a company provides additional sick pay, the rate of statutory sick pay may not be enough to enable her or her partner to take the leave they need.

One way or another, many people are forced to return to work before they are ready. They may find it hard to put on a brave face when they are at work. If you work with them, an email checking in or the offer of a coffee and a chat may help remind them that people are thinking of them and give them the opportunity to talk if they want to.

If they are having problems with their manager or HR department, they may appreciate support to seek legal advice. You could offer to attend any meetings with them or help them gather the information and paperwork they need. You could also help them to think through what 'reasonable adjustments' might be helpful. The Miscarriage Association website has a useful section on rights at work after a loss.[19]

"Returning to work was very hard. My boss knew about our fertility treatment because I had to take time off work to travel. I told her that we lost our little embryo. Her reaction and the way she engaged with me that day was just so wrong. She acted like I was a 14-year-old, who had split up with my boyfriend – cracking jokes, trying to jolly me out of my sadness. It was horrendous and so inappropriate.

What would have been better? Look me in the eye, say you are so sorry (with feeling), give me a hug and tell me earnestly that you are there for me if I need anything at all. That's it, nothing else is required. Stop talking nonsense to fill the sadness, stop trying to make me feel better. Just let me be."

Claire H

SEEING FAMILY AND FRIENDS

The person you are supporting may also be struggling to cope with other people's reactions, for example those who may not feel as if a miscarriage is something to get upset about, or may seek to reassure them in a manner they find insensitive or upsetting (see Chapter 5). Sometimes differences in opinions and reactions can come between family members and friends, which can add an extra layer of stress and sadness to the situation.

They may find it really hard to hear about, see or spend time with people who are pregnant or who have newborn babies – or even older children. This can be particularly hard with close friends, family or co-workers and it may mean they are fearful to go out or find it too difficult to see people who could otherwise offer valuable support. I go into more detail about how you can still offer support if you are in this situation in Chapters 6 and 7.

UNCERTAINTY ABOUT THE FUTURE

There may be uncertainty about what happens next. If the couple needs fertility treatment like IVF to conceive, trying again may not be a simple decision. See page 65 for more about trying again and deciding to stop trying.

"We are currently in the process of trying to decide whether or not to have another baby, and it's incredibly difficult. I really envy my friends who are making (or have made) the same decision, and all of the things they're weighing up are practical, like finances and careers. We're thinking about that stuff too, but mostly we're thinking about the 50 per cent chance of miscarriage with any new pregnancy and the emotional and physical impact that would have on us as a family. I don't want to be ill or unavailable for large portions of my daughter's early life, stuck in a cycle of endless pregnancy and miscarriage in the way my mother-in-law was. I would find it devastating if we tried and tried without success, and feel like we'd lost even more time on something that didn't work. We both want another baby, but at the moment it feels like it would be better to make a decision not to have one, than to try and fail."

Martha

CHILDLESS NOT BY CHOICE

Sadly, despite desperately wanting them, some people never have live children. This may be for physical reasons or because the trauma of a loss, or losses, means they can't keep trying.

I have used the term 'childless not by choice' in this book, but some people prefer other terms.

This pregnancy may have been their last or only attempt to have a child, and the loss may be devastating. Being childless not by choice can take a long time to come to terms with. It can mean working on trying to be happy, or at least content, with a new reality in the face of constant reminders of what could have been. Gateway Women is a global friendship and support network for women who are involuntarily childless by infertility or circumstance.[20] The Miscarriage Association has a good leaflet called *When the Trying Stops*.[21]

"The very time a woman needs endless compassion and empathy is whilst grieving the real or possible loss of motherhood. Be there and listen non-judgementally whenever she needs it."

Even if they have not stopped trying, a couple may be very anxious or uncertain about whether they will ever have a child, more so if it took them a long time to conceive, they had fertility treatment, are reaching menopause, or if this loss is the last of many. They may find it hard to voice these deep fears and anxieties and you may feel unsure about bringing the subject up.

There is still a taboo around being a childless woman, especially one who is childless not by choice. We are part of a society that feels uncomfortable about 'unfixable' things. It's spoken about even less than miscarriage. But the very time a woman needs endless compassion and empathy is whilst grieving the real or possible loss of motherhood. She may need to mourn and to talk about her pregnancies and losses too. Be there and listen non-judgementally whenever she needs it.

We mustn't forget male partners. There is perhaps less of a taboo around being a childless male, but many men desperately want children. Remaining childless isn't any easier for them to come to terms with. In fact, they may find it harder to find anyone to talk to about how they feel. Couples who are childless not by choice will be working out a new future together or trying to come to terms with this grief separately. They may appreciate having someone outside of the relationship to talk to. Couple or individual therapy may also help. Some therapists, counsellors and coaches are specifically trained to support people coming to terms with childlessness.

"There are frequent reminders of what you've lost, what you might never have, what, as a woman, you're unable to create. Pregnancy and motherhood are typically put on

a pedestal. Although it's horribly antiquated to associate having babies with womanhood, when you've failed to reproduce, despite your very best (heartbreaking, soul-destroying) efforts, you feel like a lesser human, a failure, not as good as those who've done it. It can erode self-esteem and affect the way you view yourself. It's been a while since my last loss, but the emotional scars it left me with, on top of those caused by my first miscarriage and the fairly brutal nature of the IVF process, means I'm not sure I can try again. I still dream of having a child, but not only is it physically complicated for me, there's now a psychological barrier too."

Claire

4

WHEN YOU'RE THE PARTNER

"The first miscarriage happened when we were both really young. I didn't really know how to respond, but my partner was distraught. We spoke about it a little and then within a month or two it wasn't spoken about again. When the second miscarriage happened, we were trying for a baby so it was much harder compared to the first. Again, I felt I couldn't feel the emotions as I had to be the supportive structure for my partner, who began to feel it was fate that we couldn't have kids. I didn't speak about either of the losses to anyone else. I didn't feel comfortable being the person to bring the mood down and no one I knew had experienced it."

James

This chapter is for you if you are the partner of someone who has experienced the physical loss. While we'll mostly cover how you can offer support to your partner, and what you can do if your relationship feels under strain, it's also really important that you seek out the support you need.

"Whatever you feel about your loss is valid."

If you are not a partner, you may still find it helpful to understand more about how loss can affect a relationship. Keep in mind that, in this chapter, I have used 'you' and 'your' to speak directly to partners.

BUT HOW ARE YOU?

You may have found that people do not ask about how you are coping after a pregnancy loss, but you are important too. You may recognize a lot of the emotions talked about in Chapter 2. You may not. Whatever you feel about your loss is valid. You may have had a different experience to your partner, perhaps feeling more responsibility to make decisions and offer support, putting other emotions to one side. You may have felt helpless, sidelined or traumatized by what you saw. You may not be used to seeing so much blood, or your partner in pain. You may not feel much at all and find it difficult to understand the way your partner has reacted. The lost baby may feel too abstract to you at this stage and you may feel guilty that you can't mourn in the same way as your partner. Your grief may not be at the same stage as your partner's. It may come later, or not at all. You may even feel you don't have as much 'right' to grieve as your partner. If you are not biologically connected to the baby who was lost, you may find people don't accept you as a co-parent or understand why you are grieving. This can be really hurtful.

"I was a mother losing her son, yet I didn't look like it because he wasn't in my body. As much as I wished it was me going through it rather than my wife, I was in awe of her strength at delivering our boy into the world. But we had to go through the usual rigmarole of being asked if I was Holly's 'friend' or 'sister' accompanying her to the appointments. It gets so draining always being mis-labelled in these circumstances. How hard is it to have a quick glance at the notes before walking into a room? I was there every single step of the way – every scan, every injection, every hormone-induced rage, every tear shed at the pain of treatment being delayed. I was there at the exact moment of conception and every moment after."

Kate

TALKING ABOUT YOUR LOSS

You may not be sure who to talk to about your loss. We've got more information on looking after yourself as a partner in Chapter 9, but here are some initial ideas to help you find people you can open up to.

- Some partners find that their own parents or other couples can be a good support.
- Talk to your partner too. It may help them to understand how you are really feeling, especially if you haven't shared before now.
- Sometimes, sharing something about your loss publicly, for example on social media, can help to start other, more private conversations. Be aware that this may also lead to some more insensitive comments from (usually well-meaning) people who don't fully understand.
- You may find your partner is contacted by friends who have also experienced loss. Consider contacting their friend's partner to have a chat if you feel comfortable doing so.
- Seek support from the Miscarriage Association – it offers excellent support for partners.
- If you feel it might be helpful to speak to someone else to process your feelings, you might want to seek out a counsellor (see page 38 and Useful Resources).

"I think for men in particular, the 12-week 'rule' (waiting until the first scan before you share the news) is a real problem because not only are you meant to be the 'strong, silent' type, you're meant to not talk about these things

in the first 12 weeks either, so it's two-fold. You might have lost a baby, be completely at odds with your partner because of the differing experiences of miscarriage and not be talking to anyone else about it either. Where is the release in that situation?"

Keyan

COMMON ISSUES AND DIFFICULTIES

A miscarriage, ectopic or molar pregnancy can put a strain on even the strongest of relationships. It can be even more isolating if you are struggling to communicate with or support the person who has been through this with you.

Below we'll look at some of the most common issues and difficulties that couples may face. I'm not saying these things will definitely happen to you, but all of them have happened to someone and some couples will have experienced a combination of them. It can help to read and recognize your experiences – and know you are not alone.

"If you really don't understand your partner's feelings or what you can to do help, you may feel helpless or exasperated."

DIFFERING EMOTIONS

You and your partner may feel differently about the loss, or you may have the same emotions at different times. This may be because you react differently, or because your experience wasn't the same. If you really don't understand your partner's feelings or what you can to do help, you may feel helpless or exasperated. She, or you, may feel able to move on more quickly and this can lead to frustration and sadness on the part of the person who still needs to grieve.

"In a horrible way, I needed to know that Richard was also struggling, not that I'd ever want him to go through this. But it would mean I wasn't going through it alone. I think his experience of miscarriage was different to mine, and it was very hard for him to see how devastated I was. His natural reaction was to try to help, which was wonderful but it took time for us to realize that wasn't what I needed at that stage. I needed time to grieve, and for that sadness to be recognized. I also often just needed to be held so I could cry. No words, just a hug.

We became frustrated with each other. We snapped and bickered more and stopped talking. We're getting better, talking more, and my counselling has helped. It's incredibly hard when two people are grieving at the same time, because as humans we don't grieve in the same way. And for a lot of people, this is the first time they've ever experienced grief like this. We are still together and are more content with each other now than we have been in a long time, but I can see how couples split up under the pressure of recurrent miscarriage."

Eliza

Some people experience such strong feelings of loss and grief that it can be hard for them to understand how it's possible that someone they love feels differently. There is no right way to deal with a loss, but it can be very lonely if the person you are closest to feels very differently about something so important to you.

DIFFERENT WAYS OF COPING

You and your partner may have the same kind of feelings about the loss, but cope and grieve in different ways. This can also lead to misunderstandings about how the other feels and what they need. Many women I have spoken to have said that they felt their partners didn't care about the loss, when in fact their partner had tried to keep their feelings to themselves in an attempt to help. If one of you needs to talk, and the other feels (or seems) unable to do so, it can lead to one or both of you feeling more alone.

> "Many women I have spoken to have said that they felt their partners didn't care about the loss, when in fact their partner had tried to keep their feelings to themselves in an attempt to help."

You may feel that your partner isn't dealing with things in the 'right' way. For example, you might think she is dwelling on the loss and this is not helping her. Or you may feel the opposite – that she has not given herself the time she needs to grieve and is throwing herself into something else, like work or trying to conceive another baby.

"I felt sadness and grief for a small period of time and I know we both felt it. Longer term, it affected how anxious I was about the next two pregnancies (both of which were happily fine), but the difference was that I don't think my wife felt the same way. She is admirably able to move forward!"
Gavin

ARGUMENTS

Strong emotions can make people say things they regret. You may have upset your partner, or you may feel she is being unfairly angry or pushing you away. Grief, depression, anxiety and anger can all magnify and distort other emotions, making them more difficult to deal with. You may try to explain emotions that are hard to make sense of by pointing to a 'problem' in the relationship or with the other person. In fact, things are usually more complicated than this.

ISOLATION AS A COUPLE

You may feel that you have no one to talk to about your baby and your experience of loss except each other. If you are both struggling, this can add extra strain to the relationship.

FAMILY REACTIONS

The reactions of wider family (yours or your partner's) can sometimes make things more difficult too. Family members may not understand why you are feeling the way you do. They may want to celebrate pregnancy announcements and young children and struggle with the fact you find that hard right now. Or they may say the wrong thing or act in a way you consider insensitive. This can create divisions among family members – and potentially within your relationship.

TRYING AGAIN

One of you may feel ready to try to get pregnant again sooner than the other. Some people find that sex and intimacy can be more difficult after a loss, feeling like a betrayal of the baby they lost, bringing back memories, adding extra pressure or feeling physically painful.

Loss after fertility treatment or IVF can be a particularly harsh blow and may add extra strain to a relationship already struggling to cope with the pressures of trying to conceive. If you have been paying for treatments, or will need to do so in the future, then you may have financial worries too.

If you have had a number of losses, you may have different feelings about when or whether you should stop trying to have a baby.

"My partner and I are closer and tougher as a unit than we were before our experience of loss, though it took us time to find our way. However, our experience undoubtedly impacted our relationship in other ways, too. There have been plenty of moments of tension, and our sex life definitely suffered; undergoing fertility treatment and experiencing pregnancy loss does complicated things to your relationship with your body, which in turn complicates sexual encounters. I do think it might have taken us less time to work through things if we'd sought professional help together – while I received counselling

after our third miscarriage, we never attended any
counselling together (our IVF clinic did offer it, but it was
prohibitively expensive)."
Miranda

NOT KNOWING HOW TO HELP

You may feel desperate to comfort your partner, but feel unsure
about what you can do or say to help.

> "It may feel as if it's important to 'be
> strong' for her, but sometimes this can
> backfire and make her feel that you don't
> care about the loss. It's OK to cry, or to
> share your feelings. It may help to process
> them together."

There is no right or wrong way to feel about a miscarriage, ectopic
or molar pregnancy. Your partner is dealing with her experience
in the only way she knows how. Acceptance and support can
make a huge difference. It may feel as if it's important to 'be
strong' for her, but sometimes this can backfire and make her
feel that you don't care about the loss. It's OK to cry, or to share
your feelings. It may help to process them together.

Having said that, your partner may need some additional support to help her cope with the physical side of things, and the huge hormonal changes going on in her body. Chapter 6 has suggestions for how you might be able to help, day to day.

Sometimes, asking 'How can I help?' or 'What do you need?' is a good approach. In moments of high emotion, some people may feel that if you really loved them, you should know without having to be told. It may be that they don't really know what they need, but just want you to make them feel better. It's important to keep talking.

TALKING TOGETHER

Coping together is mainly about communication. Talking things through and trying to understand and accept the other person's perspective will help you feel like you're on the same team – even if some of those feelings are different for each of you.

You may need more help to talk things through without upsetting each other. Communication can be much more difficult when both parties are coping with a loss. Here are some ideas to help:

- Finding the right time to talk can make a big difference. Some people find it easier to talk about difficult topics while on a walk or in a car, as sitting or walking side by side can sometimes feel easier than being face to face. It also makes silences and thinking time less awkward.

- Find ways that you both understand to explain how you feel. It may help to use other events or experiences you have been through together as examples.

> "It can be helpful to see your experience reflected elsewhere. It may give you hope and help you understand how you might move through it."

- Another thing that can help you describe your feelings, or understand hers, is to find and share what others have said. Charities like the Miscarriage Association and Tommy's (see Useful Resources) share lots of personal experiences online, both written and filmed. Sometimes other people can put things into words better than we can. It can also be helpful to see your experience reflected elsewhere. It may give you hope and help you understand how you might move through it.
- You might find it useful to write things down. Most people who sent me written accounts of their experiences as I was researching this book said they had found it helpful to do so.

Writing can help get your thoughts in order and give you more time to think about exactly what you want to say. If you choose to share it with your partner, you could write each other a letter or a description of your feelings and then choose a time to talk about what you have read.

- Tone of voice is important too. Remaining calm and recognizing that this conversation may be difficult for both of you will help.

- Take some time out if things are getting out of hand. Difficult emotions can make it harder to stay calm and rational. Don't blame your partner. Breathe deeply and suggest you take a pause, but don't shut the conversation down completely if your partner wants to keep talking. It could feel dismissive.

USING 'I' STATEMENTS

Feeling defensive can get in the way of solving problems. One way to try to avoid this is to use 'I' statements. 'I' statements focus on how *you feel* rather than on something the other person has *done*. They should come across as less blaming and more descriptive. 'I' statements tend to be structured something like this:

I feel [*emotion*] when [*behaviour*] because [*your thought about event or behaviour*].

Compare these statements.

'I feel lonely and upset when you don't support me in front of your family because it makes me feel as if my emotions are less important than keeping them happy.'

Vs.

'You never defend me when your mum says those things; you clearly don't care about me as much as them.'

'I feel sad when you are crying because I don't understand how you feel/I want to make you happy and I don't know how.'

Vs.

'You are always miserable but nothing I do seems to make a difference.'

'I feel upset when I don't see you crying like me because I want you to grieve in the same way as I am.'

Vs.

'You don't seem to care about the baby we lost.'

'I feel sad that our different experiences of the loss make it difficult for us to understand each other's emotions.'

Vs.

'You don't seem to care that we don't talk about what happened.'

Hopefully you can see that the 'You' statements above (the second in each pair) are focused on what your partner has done wrong. Their aim seems to be to make the other person feel bad, or to make them change.

Using 'I' statements shows you understand the difference between your own feelings and other people's behaviour. Your feelings belong to you. Even though your partner is not acting or speaking in a way you would like, you are not directly blaming them for how you feel.

Using 'I' statements can help stop the other person feeling defensive. They can help you explore your own feelings and understand how you are interacting with – and responding to – your partner's behaviour. It is a much better way to open the lines of communication.

It's OK to be open about what you are trying to do when using 'I' statements. You can even say something like, 'I want to try to talk about our feelings and actions when it comes to our loss, but I don't want to sound as if I am blaming you or trying to make you feel bad. I'm going to try and put what I want to say into words, but it might not come out right first time.'

AMY AND KEYAN'S EXPERIENCE

Finding Ways to Communicate after Multiple Miscarriages

Amy's experience

Around the second and third loss, we were starting to miss each other in our grief and I can now see how easy it would be for a couple to spin off in different directions when going through something like this. He'd often get home to find me in tears, and I started to feel guilty for always being on such a downer, but angry too that he didn't seem as bothered about it all. Trying to move me on felt dismissive and minimizing. I was realizing I wasn't just a bit sad, I was traumatized.

Meanwhile, he was realizing he wasn't actually over anything himself. He hadn't even begun to process it in the way I had, and that was totally understandable. He had to deal with all the practical details. He had not had time or space to grieve himself, and mistook that for having moved on.

Luckily, we recognized there was a mismatch and never stopped talking to each other. If we couldn't talk to each other, what hope was there? Incongruent grief is almost inevitable given how differently each partner experiences pregnancy and loss – one partner has a physical experience from the very beginning and the other does not. Add to that the fact that partners' feelings are often ignored by both medical professionals and friends/family, and that men in particular also have the societal expectation of being 'strong' and emotionless, and it's not surprising partners often unknowingly lock it all away.

We both had to learn to understand how the other was dealing with it and be honest if we'd accidentally hurt each other in the melee. Talking is the thing when it comes to all relationship stuff I think, and with this more than most things.

Keyan's experience

There was a moment, I think, when I questioned whether our relationship would recover from what we'd been through. So much of the time I felt we were in different places. It took time to realize why that was – the disconnect in experience means that of course you will feel different to a partner who has so clearly faced the physical experience of miscarriage. It might sound simple, but I think just talking more and being totally honest, even if that was difficult, helped us to bring ourselves back to the surface.

I think Amy recognized that disconnect far sooner than I did. She also recognized that I was not processing our losses – the trauma, the grief – and she helped eke that out of me.

We've always been a very open couple who talk about everything, but there were moments when I think we were in completely different places emotionally and it was sometimes difficult to be open about that because, for instance, I'd feel guilty that I wasn't as upset as Amy at a particular time.'

"Relationships take work, but you also have agency. You have power to find techniques and approaches to help you get through difficult times together."

RELATIONSHIP THERAPY

Some couples find it helpful to have a non-judgemental space with someone there to guide them through exploring feelings and talking openly. Therapy (sometimes called counselling) might be useful. You could do it together or individually. Maybe one partner wants to try it and the other feels there is no need or it wouldn't help. Bear in mind that if one of you feels the relationship needs some additional help, it means something isn't right. Being prepared to try can be a gesture of support and care in itself.

"Having counselling has been helpful in unpacking my responses to the miscarriage. I wonder whether joint counselling might have helped too ... having someone to talk to who we didn't feel like we were burdening with our sadness."

Rose

Relationships take work and management, but you also have agency. You have the power to find techniques and approaches to help you get through difficult times together. There are bound to be things you disagree on or feel differently about. By standing side by side and approaching this as a team, you are more likely to get through it together.

TRYING AGAIN

"We started trying again straight away, and I found the whole process horribly stressful and upsetting – the never-ending cycle of hoping and testing, the crushing disappointment each time my period arrived. One month I was six days late and convinced I was pregnant, and then got my period in a hotel room on a work trip away. I was meant to be schmoozing a client, but had to just pack up and go home, pretending I was ill, because

I felt so exhausted and worthless, like I wasn't able to do anything right."

Martha

Many couples will have to deal with the question of when (or whether) to start trying to get pregnant again. Getting pregnant soon after a previous miscarriage does not increase the likelihood of a further loss.[22] There's no need to wait if you feel ready as a couple (unless advised to for medical reasons) but not everyone does immediately. It's really important that you *both* have the space and time you need to recover from this loss and *both* feel ready to try again. There really is no way around this.

Most people's feelings about trying again will be more complicated than their feelings about trying to conceive the first time. Some people want to get pregnant as soon as possible after a loss. They may feel it will help them cope with their loss and move forward. Or they may be worried about their age or problems with their fertility. Others may not feel physically well enough, have to wait for fertility treatment or feel they are not able to cope with the anxiety and uncertainty of another pregnancy. One or both of you may just feel exhausted by the idea of going through it again – particularly if you have had a number of losses.

There are some practical considerations to take into account:

- The woman needs to have recovered from surgery, infection and treatment. It's also usually advised to wait until after any bleeding has stopped to have penetrative sex. This is to avoid infection.
- If your partner had a molar pregnancy then you are advised not to try to conceive for six months or a year after her first 'normal' hCG result.
- You may also be advised to wait before trying again if you have had an ectopic pregnancy (see page 10) or are having tests after recurrent miscarriage. You may find this time helpful to heal, grieve and come to terms with your loss, but you may find it really frustrating if you both want to get on and try to conceive another child.
- Even if you are both mentally and physically ready, it might be easier if you wait until after your partner has had at least one normal period again. The first menstrual cycle after a miscarriage can be much longer or shorter than usual, which makes it more difficult to date the new pregnancy. This may not be a problem for you and your partner, but bear in mind that some people find uncertainty around size-for-dates and whether the baby is growing, difficult to cope with after a previous loss.

If you have had fertility problems, or you are a same-sex couple, there may be even more to think about. It can also be more difficult. You may have to think about the expense or feel overwhelmed or scared about going through the whole process again. Female couples may also face the decision of who should carry the pregnancy this time. Some women may really need to get physically pregnant again, whereas others may be happy for their partner to take a turn.

Some people may find it helpful to seek out therapy to help them work through their emotions, or deal with the rollercoaster of trying again. See the section on therapy after a miscarriage on page 116.

> "After a missed miscarriage, I knew it would be really difficult for my wife to manage the emotions involved in trying to conceive again, and the anxiety of early pregnancy (if it even happened). I suggested that it might be helpful to look for some external support as she'd had counselling that helped her before. She saw my reasoning and we looked for a counsellor together and shared the cost. We talked about what happened in the sessions each week, when she was up to it, and it felt like a shared journey."
>
> Vic

SEX AND INTIMACY

Some people find sex or intimacy difficult after a loss. Your partner may feel uncomfortable with her body and need reassurance that you still find her sexy. If you are male, you may find that the pressure to conceive makes it harder to become aroused or reach orgasm. Both of you may find that feelings of guilt, memories of the loss or anxiety over the future makes intimacy more difficult.

You may decide not to put too much pressure on your time together at first. You might cuddle, massage and pleasure each other in other ways, or you might decide to have penetrative sex (if that's your thing), but not worry about actively trying for a while.

The most important thing, as always, is to talk about any problems you are having (see page 68).

"Understanding why your partner feels the way they do can help you continue to feel close and connected, even if you have different ideas about when – or whether – to try again."

The Sexual Advice Association may be able to help if you are having trouble with sex or intimacy after a loss (see Useful Resources).

Feeling differently about sex and intimacy or about trying again can put a real strain on a relationship. If you are the person who feels ready to start trying first, you may feel frustrated or impatient. It's good to recognize these feelings in yourself, but also to be aware that there is nothing to be gained from letting them show by withdrawing your affection, sulking or getting angry. It will just build up resentment and make your partner even less likely to want to be physically intimate or conceive a child with you. A truly loving and supportive approach is to respect their needs and wait until you both feel ready. That's not to say you can't talk about it, gently and lovingly. Understanding why your partner feels the way they do can help you continue to feel close and connected, even if you have different ideas about when – or whether – to try again.

If your partner is ready but you are not (or are not sure if you ever will be), you may feel guilty about making them wait and uncertain about what the future holds. But if you don't feel ready, you are making the right decision. Trying to conceive and going through a pregnancy after a loss can be challenging and you both need to feel strong enough to cope.

The Miscarriage Association has a good leaflet called *Thinking About Another Pregnancy*.[23] There is also a good chapter on trying again (or not) in Petra Boynton's book *Coping with Pregnancy Loss*.[24] It may help for you both to read them if you need additional support.

STOPPING TRYING

"After our third miscarriage, we were heartbroken. Richard was determined we'd never go through it again. After a time, we decided that we'd give things one more try. We took the final three cycles of clomiphene, but didn't get pregnant. At our first IVF appointment we found out we were unexpectedly pregnant, but lost that baby too. We're probably still going to go through IVF in a few months time, just so we don't have the 'what if' question hanging over us. But one more miscarriage, and that's it. That's our line."
Eliza

At some point one or both of you may decide you can't keep trying. Stopping trying for a much-wanted child is always going to be a really hard decision. It may be even harder if it means you will have no living children.

You may find you feel differently to your partner and you both make and unmake the decision a few times. It's really important to keep talking. You may feel confident in your choice, or you may take a while to accept the decision and what it means for you and your partner or family. You may need to grieve for what might have been. Some people experience a sense of relief that the uncertainty is over, even if it is not in the way they wanted it to be.

The Miscarriage Association has a good leaflet called *When the Trying Stops*.[25] If stopping trying means you will be childless not by choice, you and your partner may find it helpful to have a look at the Fertility Network's section on life without children.[26]

5

TALKING ABOUT MISCARRIAGE

"I dislike framing a loss using 'at least': 'At least you know you can get pregnant', 'At least it happened early on in the pregnancy', 'At least you're still young', etc. I understand the impulse to try to put a positive spin on something sad, but I've always found this a particularly unhelpful response, not least because it suggests a hierarchy of grief. Grief is illogical – everyone has the right to be sad about their loss(es), regardless of the circumstances, and it isn't necessarily a relief to be reminded that it could have been 'worse' in some way."

Miranda

It can be hard to find the right words to talk about miscarriage. Everyone has different experiences and may not feel the same about what happened. You have no shared memories of the person lost to find comfort in together. You may worry that you will say the wrong thing and feel it would be better to keep silent.

Acknowledgement is important. Most people say that they find it hard if people ignore their loss or act as if nothing has happened.

"It's really hard to just be with someone in grief or anger, to recognize things are really hard and that there are no easy solutions. But this is often what people need."

Feelings of shame, guilt, grief and anger are exacerbated by silence, isolation and misunderstanding. If you don't say anything, the person may assume you don't care, or that you don't think their loss is worth mentioning.

You may really want to help, but are scared of making things worse. Or perhaps you think there is no point in saying something if you can't 'solve' anything or come up with something insightful and new. It's really hard to just be with someone in grief or anger, to recognize things are really hard and that there are no easy solutions. But this is often what people need.

SUPPORTING A YOUNG PERSON

You may be in a position of trust with a young person who has confided in you. They may have planned their pregnancy, or it may have been unplanned or even unwanted. Whatever the situation, they may still be feeling complex feelings of loss and uncertainty, and feel relief as well as grief. They may be feeling isolated because they are unable to talk to their parents, and/or are without the support of a long-term partner. Talking to you and having your support could make a real difference.

It isn't just the woman herself who experiences a loss. Perhaps you are supporting the partner of someone who has had the miscarriage. Many partners don't have the opportunity to talk about their feelings and may feel they have 'less right' to do so. Female partners may find they are not accepted as co-parents and do not have their grief acknowledged, which can be really hurtful.

You don't need to say much. It may be enough to start a conversation and make space for them to talk if and when they feel able. After that, being there to listen may well be enough. If you're not sure, say less and listen more.

"The most difficult thing was when people, always those who had children, kept their distance from me. I know they

did it to try to protect me, but it made me feel isolated, broken and worthless at a really vulnerable time of my life. I felt that some people treated me like a glass doll, who was fragile and might shatter at any point. And I think at times I did shatter, and that's OK. But some people are so frightened of upsetting us or saying the wrong thing that they withdraw. For me, this isolation was far more difficult to deal with than anything they could have said."
Eliza

Admitting that you don't know what to say is better than saying nothing. A simple, 'I'm so sorry for your loss' or 'I'm really sorry, I don't know what to say but I'm thinking of you' can be enough. If someone doesn't want your sympathy or support, or needs some space, all they need to say is 'Thank you, but I'm actually OK' or similar. At least you will know you tried.

If they do want to talk, these simple words give them space to open up or to start a longer conversation, now or in the future.

"I would have liked close friends and family to talk to me about my daughter. To acknowledge that we had lost a baby. Because we lost her at 21 weeks a lot of people thought it was 'just a miscarriage'. One of the worst things for me was the confusion I felt. I felt like a mother; I had given birth. People didn't know what to say so, apart from

one or two very brave close friends, they said nothing. It was such a very lonely time."
Jen

A NOTE ABOUT LANGUAGE

"Is it naïve for us all to appreciate that two people may have similar experiences, but for one person it is 'baby loss' and for the other person it is 'pregnancy loss'?"
Esther

You may be worried about making things worse by referring to the loss in unhelpful terms. This is an understandable concern. Some women prefer 'pregnancy loss', others 'baby loss'. Some will refer to an embryo or foetus, others to a baby. Those who have to go through labour to deliver a tiny baby with no heartbeat may find there is no language to refer to something that didn't feel like a miscarriage, but was not quite a stillbirth.

"It is not just a matter of biology or viability, of the stage or quality of cell division and development. This is a personhood built from the power of their parents' love, hope, dreams, imagination and future plans."

In the absence of a word in English that is more than a medical term to describe a life or potential life before 24 weeks gestation – a being who is already a person to those who love and hope for them – most people who have experienced loss seem to use the term 'baby'. But the best rule of thumb is to take your cue from the language the person you are supporting uses. If they use 'baby', you should too. If they have a name for their little one, use that. If they are more comfortable with 'embryo', 'foetus' or another term, use this.

Some find it difficult to square the term 'baby' with a pro-choice position, while still recognizing grief after a loss. Some feel able to accept that the loss is that of a baby whether through termination or through miscarriage, ectopic or molar pregnancy – and that the personhood (or not) of the foetus is not the only factor involved. It isn't simple. What is lost may be a fully formed embryo or baby, needing only more time to grow. Or it may be a baby-shaped hope. It is not just a matter of biology or viability, of the stage or quality of cell division and development. This is a personhood built from the power of their parents' love, hope, dreams, imagination and future plans.

FINDING THE WORDS

"I think the single thing that I would have liked is for more people to ask me about my losses and experiences –

I know this isn't the case for everyone, but for me it was really important to talk about what I was going through, and I would have welcomed the opportunity to do this, but I was often wary of bringing it up myself. I've grown more open over the years and found it very rewarding; openness seems to beget openness, and it's helped me feel less alone."

Miranda

It can be very isolating for someone to live through a difficult experience that is unacknowledged by those around them. Not only do they lose out on support and a chance to talk about it, but they may start to question their own responses. This adds an extra layer of confusion to their emotions and may prevent or delay the process of working though and accepting them. They may start to give your silence their own meaning, wondering if you don't actually care or if you think less of them for being upset.

"It's better to have too much than too little – for someone to say, 'Thanks, but I've got good support around me' to lots of people offering their sorrow, love and support, than to be alone and desperate for someone to acknowledge their experience."

Even if they actually feel OK about what happened, it can feel odd if people around them know what happened but don't mention it at all.

You may think they have enough other support – but you don't know what is going on behind closed doors. It's better to have too much than too little – for them to say, 'Thanks, but I'm doing OK and I've got good support around me' to lots of people offering their sorrow, love and support, than to be alone and desperate for someone to acknowledge their experience.

The longer you don't say anything, the harder it is. It doesn't take much to acknowledge what has happened and let people know you are thinking of them.

HELPFUL PHRASES

Everyone is different and will respond to things in their own way, so I can't give you a foolproof list of what to say. What is appropriate will also depend on your relationship with the person you are supporting. But I've talked to a lot of women who have experienced miscarriage and these are some of the things people have said that they have found helpful:

- 'I'm so sorry for your loss.'
- 'I'm here to talk if you want to.'
- 'I'm not sure what to say, but I am here to talk if you need it.'

- 'Sorry things are so hard. I'm here if you need anything.'
- 'I'm thinking of you.'
- 'I don't know a lot about [miscarriage], but I'm here to listen if you want to talk about it.'
- 'I'm so sorry things are so hard; I wish there was more I could do. I'm always here for you.'
- 'It's OK to grieve/to give yourself time to grieve.'
- 'Let yourself feel whatever you are feeling. I am here for you.'

"If you are pregnant and are worried they might not want to see you, or concerned you might make things worse, it's best to acknowledge it, however awkward it might feel."

I've mentioned how hard it can be for someone who has just experienced a loss to spend time with pregnant women, or with those who have children. If you are worried they might not want to see you, or concerned that you might make things worse, it's best to acknowledge it, however awkward it might feel. Perhaps you might say something like, 'I know it may be difficult for you to see me right now, but I am thinking of you and sending my love.'

If talking really does feel too hard, then sending a message, card, flowers or food shows you are thinking of them (see page 108).

Even though your experiences may be different, they may find it helpful to hear your own story of loss, if you feel comfortable sharing it.

UNHELPFUL THINGS TO SAY

There are some things that can be upsetting, even when meant well. For example, I have never met anyone who was genuinely comforted by any statement starting with 'at least'. Try not to 'solve' the problem or minimize the person's feelings. This can make it harder for them to talk about their loss, for fear of sounding ungrateful for what they do have.

Avoid comments like:

- 'At least it was early.'
- 'At least you know you can still get pregnant.'
- 'At least you have other children.'
- 'It was obviously not meant to be.'
- 'It wasn't a real baby/it was only a ball of cells.'
- 'It may have been for the best.'
- 'You'll have other children.'
- 'They never used to even say you were pregnant before two missed periods.'

And of course, anything that implies blame is completely out of the question. Even off-the-cuff or flippant comments can be really hurtful. It's natural to try to find a reason as it means it may be avoidable in the future, but this implies the person did something wrong this time. Women often feel incredibly and irrationally guilty after a loss anyway, despite the fact it was very unlikely to have been caused by anything they did or did not do.

Examples of comments that may imply blame include:

- 'Maybe you didn't wait long enough before getting pregnant again.'
- 'Really look after yourself this time.'
- 'Maybe you waited too long to start trying.'
- 'Try to think positively; stress won't help.'
- 'You walked ten miles? That might explain it then.'

People who are childless not by choice or struggling to have a child through fertility treatment or after multiple losses, have told me they don't like it when people ask if they have thought about adoption.

"She asked if I'd thought of adoption – one of the top ten things NOT to say to someone who's going through IVF or has experienced pregnancy loss. Of course I've thought about it. Adoption can be hugely rewarding and

it's something we'll consider, but the way she mentioned it
made it sound like a quick fix, a substitute for the baby I'd
just lost, the baby I might never be able to have."
Claire

Other things that people who are childless not by choice find
difficult to hear is any suggestion that they are 'lucky' not to
have children – even if they are meant in jest. Again, these
are comments that try to put a positive spin on things, to fix
something that may be unfixable.

- 'But you are so lucky not to have kids – you can sleep in
  and go travelling, sounds amazing.'
- 'Kids aren't all they are cracked up to be; have one
  of mine.'

IF YOU ACCIDENTALLY SAY
THE WRONG THING

Saying the wrong thing is a lot of people's worst nightmare.
They would rather say nothing than risk getting it wrong. I
hope this book has managed to convince you that taking
the risk and saying *something* is usually better.

If you are worried you have said the wrong thing or
accidentally hurt someone, try to own it and apologize.

This will mean a lot more to the people involved than saying something hurtful and then disappearing, or failing to mention it again. If you really feel unable to say something face-to-face, it's still worth sending a message, along the lines of:

'I've been worrying that I accidentally made things worse by saying X. I'm so sorry; I didn't mean it like that at all. I just wanted to help, but I was feeling awkward and it came out wrong.'

If the person doesn't immediately get back to you with reassurance or forgiveness, give it time. Apologizing was still the best course of action, even if the person doesn't feel able to acknowledge it right now.

TALKING ABOUT RECURRENT MISCARRIAGE

"With recurrent miscarriage, you are often conscious your constant 'drama' might be getting wearing and sympathy is running out. Our closest friends never made us feel like we were a drain on their emotional energy."

Amy

People who have had multiple losses say that the support they receive usually diminishes after each loss. They wondered if people felt they were 'used to it' now. In fact, the opposite is often the case. People who suffer multiple losses need even more love and care each time. Many need acknowledgement that they are going through something incredibly hard.

Take each loss as seriously as the last. You can start the conversation in the same ways as we've mentioned above, by saying something like:

- 'I'm so sorry this has happened again.'
- 'This must be so incredibly hard for you; I'm thinking of you a lot.'
- 'I'm so sorry for your loss.'
- 'I can't pretend to imagine how awful this must be for you, but I'm here and I love you.'

Multiple losses can be a real strain on couples. One or both of them may find it helpful to have someone else to talk to.

"As we have been quite open about the miscarriages, I think people have felt able to ask how the recurrent miscarriage tests are going, which I have found supportive. Some people have said well-meaning things such as, 'Next time will be better for you', which I don't find helpful as there is a real possibility for us that things might not be fine, but I know people mean to be reassuring and want to make us feel better. Personally, I have found it more supportive when people just

*acknowledge how awful things must be and ask how
we are."*
Sally

CONTINUING THE CONVERSATION

Saying, 'I'm sorry for your loss' is a good start. If you are close
to the people involved, the examples above are ways to start
the conversation. Once you've said something, it's much easier
to keep talking.

Even if you are more distantly connected, there are ways
that you can continue to show support and sensitivity. (Also see
Chapters 6 and 7.)

- Try to keep checking in with the person you are
  supporting, especially on important dates or times that
  may be upsetting (a pregnancy announcement, a newborn
  in the family or office, Mother's Day or Father's Day).
- Give them space and time to talk – suggest going for a
  walk, or meeting for a coffee. It can sometimes be easier
  to talk when driving or walking side by side.
- Listen to what they have to say, reflect their emotions and
  acknowledge how they are feeling. Remember, you don't
  have to solve anything.

- They may find it helpful to talk about what happened, to have some space to cry and to remember their little one.
- They may look for reassurance that it wasn't anything they did. (Give it to them – statistics show it's very unlikely to be anything they did or didn't do.)
- They may not want to talk about their loss at all. Some people find that knowing that they can is enough.

TALKING ABOUT LOSS TO THE WIDER WORLD

"The pain of pregnancy loss and infertility is a wound, deep inside you, invisible to everyone else. The trouble is, it's not easy for anyone to talk about. A taxi driver asked if I had children when I was on my way to the hospital for counselling after my first loss. I just said no, although I feel like I've had two children I didn't get to meet. Afterwards, I thought, why couldn't I be more honest? I wanted to save him from feeling awkward, I suppose. In the dry cleaners, a week after a failed IVF cycle, a woman asked me when I was due. I had a bloated stomach thanks to weeks of hormones and enlarged follicles, but there was no baby. Again, I tried not to cause embarrassment, made a joke about the way

my clothes were hanging. Walking home, I wished I'd told
the truth. It might have made her think twice next time."
Claire

A chapter on talking about miscarriage wouldn't be complete without something about talking to the wider world.

The experience above, plus those of many others who have shared their stories, show that loss in pregnancy isn't something we think about. Nor do we discuss fertility problems or the possibility of being childless not by choice. If we haven't experienced it, we may not even consider it happening to others.

"Part of offering support is knowing about, and being more sensitive to, these experiences as you go about your daily life."

We teach people how *not* to get pregnant and worry about scaring those who are with the possibility of loss – something that must be a hangover from the days when pregnant women were considered particularly delicate, needing to be wrapped in cotton wool and shielded from everyday horrors.

Even if we go through it ourselves, we don't always talk about our experiences. The silence surrounding the issue makes many people think it 'should' be kept private or that they 'shouldn't' be feeling these difficult emotions.

Part of offering support is knowing about, and being more sensitive to, these experiences as you go about your daily life. Be aware that there may be more going on in someone's life than appears on the surface. Be careful with flippant comments or jokes about children or childlessness.

You don't have to have experienced a loss yourself to share and amplify the words of those who have. We need more people who are prepared to talk about loss openly, to bring it out of the shadows and into daily conversation.

Look for and support Baby Loss Awareness Week (#BLAW) – usually 9–15 October.[27] Amplify those talking about miscarriage, ectopic and molar pregnancy on social media with a retweet or a share. Talk about your own experience if you feel comfortable doing so. Educate yourself online.

"A better general understanding of what miscarriage can involve would make a huge difference to so many. The more we talk about it, the more likely it is that mental health assessments post-loss become standard, for both women and their partners, and appropriate support routinely offered. The more likely it is that friends, family and co-workers understand exactly how traumatic baby loss can be and take it seriously, no matter how many weeks. The

more likely it is that those experiencing it don't feel shame or guilt for being so affected by it, or isolated because they assume nobody else feels the same way. The tone of most of the messages I received, and continue to receive, after writing so much about baby loss, is just that: thank God I'm not alone."

Amy

6

PRACTICAL MATTERS: WHAT CAN YOU DO?

"The best kind of support is when someone tries to empathize with my situation, doesn't expect too much of me during difficult times, doesn't hold it against me when I need to be by myself, listens without trying to fix anything, shows awareness when discussing pregnancy and babies, doesn't urge me to think positively (it's not that easy!) or relay miracle stories about the birth of their supposedly infertile friend's son or daughter (our issues are probably not the same)."
Claire

By now, you should have a better idea of what the person you are supporting is going through, what they might need and how you can talk to them about their loss. In this chapter, we'll think about what else you can do.

"I am part of a singing group and in the middle of lockdown we had a Zoom call just to connect socially. About ten minutes before the call, the guy who runs it rang to pre-warn me that there may be a few newborn babies, as three members had just given birth. It showed that someone cared about how I would feel enough to make sure I wasn't put on the spot and taken by surprise. It also ensured that I could decide what to do in advance and prepare myself if I still wanted to join, which I did."

Esther

Your supporting role will depend on your relationship with the person and what else is going on in your own life, but you can always do or say something that will help, even in a small way. Many small acts of kindness and care can add up to a great deal. Staying patient, being kind and keeping an open mind will go a long way.

DAY-TO-DAY SUPPORT

"My best friend asked to come and see me instead of saying, 'Let me know when you're up to having visitors' like every other person did. I don't think anyone who sent me that type of message actually came to see me as I never

felt like I wanted to be the one to message them to say, 'Can you come and see me?'"
Gemma

BE PROACTIVE

It's easy to say to someone, 'Let me know if there's anything I can do' and feel as if you've done your bit by leaving the ball in their court. It can sometimes help to be more proactive in your offer of help or companionship. Make specific suggestions, while also recognizing that things are hard and the person you are trying to support may not feel up to seeing people. Remember that feelings change and while they may not feel up to company at first, this might be different the following week, so don't just ask once.

Here are some examples of being specific and proactive:

- 'Are you up for a visit today? I'd really like to pop over, even if it's just for a quick hug – but I want to make sure you feel up to it.'
- 'A small group of us are going for a drink/a coffee/lunch/ dinner if you fancy joining us. I know things are hard at the moment, though, so no pressure. But it would be good to see you if you feel up to it. No need to decide immediately.'

- 'I'm going to the shop/walking the dog/taking the children to the park in an hour or so. Can I pick you anything up/ take your dog/take your child out too?'
- 'I'm going for a walk at lunchtime/in your area if you fancy coming along.'
- 'Is there anything specific I can do to help you right now?'

"Little things have really meant a lot – a friend bringing round flowers, or cooking us dinner one night shortly after a miscarriage, or just offering to come round and have a cup of tea. Even if I didn't take up the offer, it was a great comfort to know that it was there."
Miranda

SEND A CARD OR GIFT

A card or gift helps remind someone that you care when they are going through a difficult time. The Miscarriage Association sells specific cards for people who have been through pregnancy loss,[28] but you could send any card that shows love and sympathy. They also offer 'Virtual hugs' – cards you can download to your phone and send. You could also send flowers, food, pampering stuff or anything else the person might like. Someone I know really appreciated a box of cheese.

"Nobody treated us as though we had lost our daughter. When our son was born we were deluged with cards and gifts. I resented it, to be honest. Where were all of you before?"

Jen

DROP ROUND SOME MEALS

This is another way of reminding someone you care. Food and eating may be the last thing on the person's mind, but a food parcel or some pre-cooked meals can mean one less thing to think about.

"A friend left a fruit pie outside our door with a note. I wasn't ready to see anyone, but this really made me feel loved."

Rose

REMEMBER THEIR BABY

"Friends and family sent gifts to remember Lumi by. He has two stars named in his memory amongst other thoughtful keepsakes, such as baubles for the Christmas tree, so he can be remembered and included every Christmas."

Emma

Another way to show you are thinking of them is to do something to remember the baby they have lost and to recognize their existence. What is meaningful to the person you are supporting may depend on different social, cultural and religious factors, their own preferences and tastes and the meaning for them of this particular pregnancy.

Some things people have appreciated include:

- Naming a star in their child's memory.
- Giving a piece of remembrance jewellery. Some people like forget-me-not motifs, but there are all sorts of memorial items available. Keep it simple if you are not sure of their taste.
- Planting a tree or giving a plant for their garden. One woman was very moved by a forget-me-not plant, grown from seed.
- A Christmas tree decoration in memory.
- A donation to a miscarriage or baby loss charity in memory.

The Miscarriage Association has a useful page on marking a loss, too.[29]

"As time went on, my friend sought to find a way to remember her lost baby, and have something tangible

to hold on to. I found it really helpful to find a piece of
memorial jewellery and suggested she look for one for her
baby. She was definitely a lot brighter when she had chosen
and ordered a necklace. She also began to write down
poetry – I guess you'd call them inspirational quotes – so
if I ever come across any, I send them over to her."

Leah

OFFER ADDITIONAL HELP

There may be other things you can do, depending on your
relationship with the person. This might include:

- Helping them to unsubscribe from marketing and emails
  aimed at expectant parents. Emails will usually need to be
  unsubscribed from individually, so they would need to give
  you access to deal with them. See Useful Resources for
  links on how/where to do this.
- Looking after their other children, if they have any.
- Telling others about the loss, if they would like you to.
- Doing housework and other daily tasks they may not feel
  up to.
- Just being there and keeping them company.
- Helping them to feel safe, loved and comforted – for
  example, by making sure they have space to wrap up

warm, cuddle something they love, drink something hot and perhaps watch something they enjoy.

"Sometimes, writing can make it easier for people to share how they are feeling."

SUPPORT FROM AFAR

You may not be in a position to offer face-to-face support or practical help with housework, but there is still a lot that you can do from afar. Care packages and presents can be posted, messages of support and love can be sent via message or email. The person you are supporting will appreciate knowing that you are just a phone or video call away if they need you. Sometimes, writing can make it easier for people to share how they are feeling.

"It helped that I didn't see her face-to-face because she knew she could contact me when she needed, but she wasn't surrounded by my sympathy on a daily basis. I know she wanted to try to come to terms with her loss as quickly as possible."
Leah

ACCESSING FURTHER SUPPORT

The person you are helping may need some extra care from experts, peer supporters or others who have been through a similar experience. Finding some additional sources of support may help you both, especially if the person is very reliant on you and has not been able to talk to anyone else about their loss. Your role may be to make them aware of these options, or help them access them.

Some people find it helpful to talk to someone they are close to about the experiences they are having, so once they are accessing further support, check in with them to find out how they are getting on.

ONLINE SUPPORT AND HELPLINES

"The online baby loss community really was my only support in the months that followed."
Gemma

Group support, online communities and helplines can facilitate peer support and reduce isolation.

Many people who experience a loss find it helpful to hear from, and talk to, people who have been through something similar. Sometimes talking anonymously or to people they don't know can feel easier too. It may help to share some of these links with the person you are supporting if they have not found them already.

Online communities: There are a lot of online support communities. I would recommend looking for official groups that are safe and well moderated, but there are hundreds of unofficial groups on Facebook, or based around hashtags on Twitter or Instagram. Some of these are very well established. I have included some examples in Useful Resources. They can usually provide support for partners too. Even if you have not been affected personally by a loss, you may find it helpful to look at some of the posts to understand more about how people feel and what they have been through.

Some are public groups; if they are private, it means the person can post anonymously or others can't see what they post. Different communities will be set up in different ways, but most will have a guidance section to help you understand what they offer and how to use them. The Miscarriage Association also has a good page to help people decide what kind of online support is right for them.[30] This is in the Useful Resources section too.

"The Facebook group is a wealth of information and support and is so powerful because even though there is

no one who has experienced exactly the same as you, or the people you are supporting, there is always someone who has had a similar experience."
Leah

Helplines: The Miscarriage Association, the Ectopic Pregnancy Trust and Tommy's all have helplines staffed by people who will listen and understand (see Useful Resources). They will be happy to talk to the person you are supporting, and to you in your supportive role, to help you understand what you can do. There may be an option to communicate via live chat and email, if you prefer.

GROUP SUPPORT

"I plucked up the courage to start attending the monthly open support meetings and met many bereaved parents with whom I could talk openly about all my feelings surrounding the loss."
Emma

A number of charities run support groups for people affected by miscarriage, ectopic pregnancy or molar pregnancy. Sometimes these are run face to face, but at other times they are online via video chat.

Attending a support group may feel daunting, but a lot of people find them really useful and speak of a 'weight being lifted' after spending time with people who really understand. Listening to the feelings of others can sometimes help people understand their own emotions better too.

Here are some things that may help the person you are supporting attend a group, if this is what they want:

- Online groups may feel easier at first. There is an extra layer of 'protection' given by the screen, and they can leave at any time.
- They can try a number of different groups to find one that feels right for them.
- They do not have to talk if they don't want to, but can just sit and listen to others for as long as they need.
- If attending online, they may need help to find the right link and get set up – sometimes little things can feel overwhelming when you're struggling.
- They may like you to go with them to a face-to-face group, either to stay or just to accompany them to the door.

THERAPY

Many people who have experienced a loss find some kind of therapy helpful, whether they have a mental health problem or not. A therapist can help someone understand more about themselves and offer coping strategies. Space to talk openly about how they feel, without judgement or criticism, can really help too.

See page 38 for more information on helping to access therapy.

7

ONGOING SUPPORT

For many people (but not everyone) their loss or losses will always be a part of their lives in some way. It may be something they only really think about occasionally, perhaps on the anniversary of a due date or loss. Or it may become a larger part of their identity and the way they make sense of their journey to try to have a family. If they are going through fertility investigations, are trying to conceive naturally or are childless not by choice, then they may have to manage constant painful reminders of what has happened or is still happening to them. Recognizing this and being sensitive to it can make a big difference.

Of course, some people will want to put their loss behind them, so not all of the suggestions in this chapter will be relevant to everyone. Having said that, most of them are the kind of basic sensitivities that most people will appreciate regardless of how they remember their loss or losses.

KEEP CHECKING IN

"It's been helpful when people have continued checking in on us. Because of the infertility, we knew it wouldn't be easy to get pregnant again (not that getting pregnant is any 'cure' for the grief). I think quite a few people thought that if they backed off for a couple of months, we'd be pregnant again and everything would be fine. But those months turned into years with further miscarriages, and we wouldn't have been able to carry on without the support of the people who walked alongside us during that time."

Eliza

If you know the person you are supporting is going through medical investigations and has specific dates for appointments and results, consider sending a simple message beforehand asking how they are and whether they need anything.

"Every person and every loss is unique, but your understanding of how they have managed so far will help you to think about what they need."

If you know someone has had a loss and that they are trying to conceive again, it's worth continuing to check in. This can give them an opportunity to share any uncertainties or anxieties in the early days of trying to conceive and about pregnancy after loss.

It may also help to show your support if someone else in your friend or family group announces a pregnancy or a birth. See the sections that follow for more detail on thinking about what, or how, you share. It's also worth bearing in mind that they may struggle throughout the pregnancy of someone they are close to. Don't forget them if you are also celebrating other people's good news.

"The first loss hurt even more as my sister-in-law was blossoming in her pregnancy. My family focused on her and for nine months I grieved alone."
Vicki

The person may be worried about being a burden, or think that everyone assumes they are 'over it' by now. When you check in regularly, they know that you are still thinking of them and it can help to reassure them it's OK to still be finding things hard. You may be uncertain about whether they want to be 'reminded' of their loss, but even if it's something they want to put behind them, a sensitive message is still likely to be appreciated.

Every person and every loss is unique, but your understanding of how they have managed so far will help you to think about what they need. Here are some examples of messages that have helped other people:

- 'Hey there, how are things? I think your first appointment with the clinic is this week. I really hope it goes OK and you are feeling OK about it. I'm here to talk if you need anything.'
- 'Hi, I heard [name]'s news and wanted to send a message to make sure you are doing OK with it. I'm here if you need anything or want to chat. Sending lots of love.'
- 'Hey, just wanted to see how things were. I know the time I found most difficult was a few months after my miscarriage, so wanted to check in with you.'

Or even something as simple as ...

- 'Hi, how are you doing? Hope things are going OK.'

ANNIVERSARIES AND SPECIAL DAYS

"Weeks went by and things went back to 'normal'. No one really spoke about the loss and I gradually felt lonelier and lonelier. I was approaching the due date of our baby

and no one seemed to remember, including my husband.
I honestly have never felt so low in my life."
Gemma

Many people who experience a loss will remember the due date of their lost baby. Their baby's birthday, or the date of their loss, may also be something they never forget. These dates can be meaningful times to remember and mourn, but they can also be emotional and upsetting – times of intense grief. These dates are not usually known to many, and can easily go unnoticed and forgotten by everyone except the mother and maybe her partner. Feeling as if everyone else is 'back to normal' and no one remembers or grieves for their lost baby except them can be very isolating.

If you know when the due date would have been, or the date of their loss, it may help to put a reminder in your calendar so you remember to get in touch.

Mother's Day and Father's Day can also be a difficult time, especially for those people who are going through recurrent losses or have no live children. It's worth being sensitive about what you share when celebrating these days. If appropriate, you may wish to help them unsubscribe from Mother's Day-specific marketing emails etc. More and more companies are becoming sensitive to this and giving people the option to opt out. Some people, but not all, may still identify as a mother of the babies they have lost, and if they have shared this with you, would appreciate a note or card recognizing this.

Other days when the person may need extra support can include those often celebrated with family, such as Christmas, Eid or other religious festivals, and days when there is a big news story about a newborn, for example a royal or celebrity baby.

"I grieved all over again when my menopause started shortly after I turned 40. That was it. Never going to be a mum to a living child. Mother's Day was the kicker. My miscarriage was in 2000. My mum died in 2014. The first Mother's Day after mum died, I felt lost. I have no place in Mother's Day at all. I don't belong. These days I just stay away from social media on Mother's Day. I stay away from my family. All my sisters have children. Some now have grandchildren. Not all of them know, to be honest, but I shied away from talking about my miscarriage when I was unsupported by close friends at the time."

Bernadette

Here are some examples of messages that have helped other people:

- 'Just wanted to say I'm thinking of you and [your partner]. I know this time last year was really hard for you. I hope you are doing OK. I'm here if you need anything, but also understand if it's not something you want to remember or talk about.'

- 'Hey, I know it was around now that [your baby/your little one/'name'] would have been due, so I hope it's OK to get in touch and send you my love. I'm thinking of you and of [baby name/them].'

NEWS ABOUT PREGNANCY, BABIES AND CHILDREN

"From the time I returned to work after the Easter holidays until I finally fell pregnant (with a miscarriage in between to deal with), EIGHT colleagues announced pregnancies. Only one of them came to tell me face-to-face, which I appreciated. I was genuinely happy for her and gave her a huge hug. She must have been so worried about telling me. The other announcements were all online or in work emails and I found it terribly hard to deal with. I would have appreciated just a little tact and maybe a personal face-to-face heads up. I would have found it marginally easier to deal with."

Emma

This is something everyone should bear in mind, regardless of whether they know someone who has experienced a loss. It's likely that someone at work, in your friendship group or social media circle has gone through miscarriage, ectopic or molar pregnancy, even if it is not public knowledge.

Of course, you will be excited to share your joy – but a little tact and, in some cases, restraint can make a big difference to those who are struggling. Here are some things to think about when it comes to sharing news about pregnancy, birth and children:

- If you plan to announce a pregnancy (whether at work via email, on social media or in a messaging group) and you know someone who will see it has experienced a loss, get in touch with them first to let them know. This will give them a little more time to prepare – and shows you are thinking of them. If possible, let them know face-to-face. The same applies to a new baby.

- Think about whether you need to post regular updates about your pregnancy or new baby on social media.

- Don't go out of your way to hide a pregnancy and baby news, especially if you are close to the people involved. This will just make them feel more isolated. Talk to them sensitively and give them space and time to adjust. If their loss is really recent, you may consider delaying your own announcement by a few weeks.

- News or discussion about how easy, annoying or inconvenient it was to get pregnant quickly can be upsetting to those struggling with fertility issues.
- If they feel unable to respond, get in touch or see you, don't take it personally. It may feel hurtful but they are probably struggling with difficult and conflicting emotions and dealing with it in the best way they know how. They may feel happy for you but also sad for themselves, jealous of your luck and guilty that they feel this way. Try to understand, even if you feel you would have dealt with things differently.

COPING WITH CHANGES IN YOUR FRIENDSHIP

"There was one group of friends, most of whom had children by the time of my first miscarriage. I made a big effort to be part of their lives, texting them to congratulate them on pregnancies I was genuinely happy about, and asking them about their children. But they were in another world and didn't seem to want to talk to me, so I felt like an outsider looking in through a window. One of them didn't invite us to her child's baptism, which really hurt. I know that some people who have experienced miscarriage really struggle with events like this, but it felt as though she'd

127

cast me as this bitter, jealous woman without really talking to me. I needed them to still see me as Eliza, rather than defining me completely by my miscarriages. I needed to feel that I still belonged in their group/community, even when they had kids and I didn't. But maybe that's not always possible."

Eliza

"Someone once said to me, 'My life has got smaller since my miscarriages' and I have never forgotten it. That simple line captured the pain of changing relationships and drifting friendships."

Friendships and family relationships can be affected by loss, recurrent loss and childlessness. People report feeling left out or sidelined as friends and family have children, with a feeling that others are moving on without them. Others say they feel like an outsider who no longer has anything in common with the people they have always been closest to. They may really want to continue with the friendship, but find it too difficult to be around people who are pregnant or who have children. Someone once said to me, 'My life has got smaller since my miscarriages' and I have never forgotten it. That simple line captured the pain of changing relationships, drifting friendships and even, for some people, a fear of going out in case they see pregnant women or newborn babies.

Friendships and relationships do evolve as life changes. It's really hard to find that, for a while, you have a lot less in common with someone you were once really close to. It isn't usually anyone's fault, but there are some things you can do to help make things easier for everyone:

- Ask them what they would find easiest right now. Despite finding things difficult, many people don't want to be defined by their experiences of loss and may appreciate being able to explain what they can and can't handle at the moment. Remember this is likely to change with time.

- Don't leave them out of events such as christenings, baby showers or birthday parties. Send a sensitive message in advance of any invitations, letting them know that the event is taking place, asking them whether they want to come along and explaining that you understand if they would prefer not to.

- Understand that if you are pregnant or have children they may have to distance themselves from you for a while. Try not to take this personally and make sure they know that you are always there if and when they want to reconnect. You may find it helpful to message saying something like, 'I know you might not want to see me right now, but I am thinking of you, and here for you whenever you are ready.'

- If they do feel able to stay in contact, make sure your conversations are not just pregnancy and baby related. Find things to do and talk about that you have enjoyed together in the past. See them without your children sometimes, if you can.

- If you don't have children and are not trying to start a family, they may find it easier to be around you. Make sure you keep in touch.

- If you and a number of your friends have children, make sure it's not all you talk about when you meet up, or over messaging groups. Find other things you all have in common and focus on them.

- People often take difficult feelings out on people they are close to. Remind yourself that it's these emotions speaking right now, not them.

- Remember that they don't want this any more than you do. They probably find it really hard that things are no longer the same between you. They may feel guilty for this as well as hating themselves for struggling with jealousy, envy or anger.

SUPPORT THE BABY LOSS COMMUNITY

Many people who go through miscarriage, ectopic or molar pregnancy want to do something to raise awareness or give back to charities who supported them. Helping them to do this can be a meaningful gesture.

You could choose to fundraise yourself for a baby loss charity – or sponsor the person you are supporting in their own efforts. Include a message of support and love with your sponsorship.

The section on talking about miscarriage more widely in Chapter 5 has more on sharing and amplifying voices in the baby loss community. Look out for Baby Loss Awareness Week in October each year.

SUPPORTING SOMEONE THROUGH PREGNANCY AFTER LOSS

"Pregnancy after loss is petrifying. The innocent assumption that a line on a test means a baby in nine months, wasn't one we could make. The thought of going through what we went through last time terrified me. It was almost enough to make me wish I wasn't pregnant. Not because I didn't want the baby, but because I didn't want the miscarriage."
Claire

TRYING TO CONCEIVE AND PREGNANCY AFTER LOSS

Trying to conceive and being pregnant after a loss can bring up complex emotions relating to previous losses and feelings and hopes for this pregnancy.

The person you are supporting may be trying to cope with a fear of never having a living child. This can be especially strong if they have been through a number of miscarriages, but any loss means someone can no longer blithely assume a pregnancy means a baby. They may worry about years of trying to conceive, pregnancy, further miscarriages and running out of time.

"The strain of waiting and enduring ongoing uncertainty about something so important and life changing, but also so tentative, can be mentally exhausting."

They may be scared of having another loss. This can cause conflicting emotions about trying to get pregnant at all. The fear of the physical and emotional pain of another miscarriage can extinguish or diminish feelings of joy in a new pregnancy. Not everyone understands this. Family and friends may express happiness and excitement. They are likely to view reassurance scans as just that, an opportunity to reassure you, rather than a moment when you are told if things are well, for now, or if everything has gone wrong, again.

Pregnancy involves a lot of waiting: waiting between ovulation and a positive pregnancy test, waiting for early scans, waiting between scans, waiting for a time when things feel as if they are on more solid ground. Even after the point where the chance of loss drops dramatically, the onus is still on the pregnant woman to measure movement and make judgements as to whether their baby is well. Many women don't feel able to fully relax until their baby is in their arms, and maybe not even then. The strain of waiting and enduring ongoing uncertainty about something so important and life changing, but also so tentative, can be mentally exhausting. Many women and their partners do endure, but often privately and without support.

They may deal with ongoing worry, analysing symptoms, checking toilet paper and fearing any 'wetness' in their underwear. Some people may try to manage this anxiety through superstition and hypervigilance.

"Every time I went to the toilet, I was scared to look at my underwear or into the toilet for fear of seeing blood or brown cervical fluid. When you think about how many times you go to the toilet every day, that's a lot of fear and anxiety to have to deal with. It wasn't just going to the toilet either; it's like I was hypersensitive and I could feel every movement that was happening down below. I'd be in the middle of a meeting or driving or chatting to someone and I'd feel some liquid come out

of me and I'd seize up and couldn't rest until I'd find a
bathroom and could have a look to make sure there was
no blood. Living in that heightened state of anxiety is
hugely problematic for a person's physical and mental
health."

Gemma

It can feel almost impossible to move on from a previous loss
when you live with the daily fear of it happening again. Some
people may also feel guilt about 'replacing' their lost baby, or
fear of forgetting them.

They may avoid bonding with their bump and the baby
inside, distance themselves from the pregnancy and resist
making plans or thinking about the future.

Scans and appointments can feel very stressful, especially
if it involves returning to the place where they had difficult
experiences previously. This may feel almost impossible for
those who had PTSD symptoms, such as flashbacks, after their
previous loss or losses.

Partners may feel even less in control, desperate for things to
go well but without even a bodily connection to the pregnancy.
They may also fear for their partner and the physical and
emotional pain she would have to cope with if things were to
go wrong.

Experiences of pre- and postnatal depression may be harder to cope with on top of feelings that they 'should' be grateful for this pregnancy, or this baby – especially after a long build up and with high expectations.

> "I found pregnancy really, really hard and hated every single minute of it. I was sick every day for almost the full nine months, and had such bad back and pelvic pain. And I felt guilty for finding it hard, because I knew I was lucky to be pregnant at all. I prevented myself from bonding with the baby, and lived in a state of constant anxiety that she would disappear. I had recurring nightmares about waking up and finding my stomach deflated. When my baby arrived safely it took a few days to properly bond with her, and I spent the first couple of months being very, very anxious. I'd stay awake staring at her, terrified that if I went to sleep she'd die."
>
> Martha

Sometimes it is not possible for partners to attend scans and medical appointments. Women may have to cope with being alone as they are told their baby has not survived. Those with previous losses have to deal with the stress of attending scans alone. Partners may miss the important bonding experience of seeing their baby on screen. This can make coping with pregnancy after a loss even more difficult.

HOW YOU CAN HELP

"I worried that the additional scans she wanted weren't really helping. I wondered if the brief amount of reassurance they gave was worth the high levels of anxiety beforehand, and the exhaustion afterwards. I did mention this to her, but in the context of being happy to support whatever she felt she needed. In the end she had extra scans at 8, 10, 15 and 17 weeks."

Vic

A small amount of early research has found that supportive care and ongoing emotional support may make a difference in preventing unexplained recurrent miscarriage.[31] The care identified included being taken seriously, listened to and empathized with, as well as additional medical support – for example, regular scans and clear information. Ideally healthcare providers would be responsible for this, but as a friend, partner or family member, you can certainly play a role in taking the person's emotions seriously, listening and empathizing. If nothing else, you may make the weeks of waiting and uncertainty a little easier to bear. Here are some ways you can help:

- You are unlikely to be able to talk the person you are supporting out of their anxiety or reduce their fears with rational arguments or statistics (although some people may briefly find statistics reassuring). Accept, recognize and reflect the person's emotions. Try not to diminish them or argue them away. It would be unusual for them not to feel anxious or unhappy at least some of the time. Sometimes reassurance may be helpful, but recognize that they are unlikely to be able to really believe things will work out this time round. This may be partly a natural protective defence mechanism, but it can still be very hard to live with.

- The person you are supporting may withdraw into herself, enduring the waiting and going through the motions of life while focused inwards on the pregnancy and difficult symptoms of the first trimester. This doesn't necessarily mean she wants to be alone or doesn't need someone to support her. Make sure you check in on how she is doing and offer her as much care as you can.

- Get in touch before scans (if you know when they are) to make sure the person you supporting knows you are thinking of them and that you are there whatever happens. Remember that scans and appointments may be anxiety-inducing in themselves, but also bring back memories of previous distress.

- Help her to get the support she needs to feel reassured at any given time. This may be extra ultrasound scans, additional midwife appointments to listen to the baby's heartbeat and trips to hospital to monitor the baby. Try to focus on what they need for reassurance, even if you feel it is unnecessary, irrational or an additional pressure on your daily lives.

- Encourage her and her partner to do things to help manage their anxiety and stay calm. This may be exercise, mindfulness, meditation, yoga or something they know relaxes them like gardening or cooking. It's unlikely to make the anxiety go away completely, but can help reduce stress in the short-term and may make each day easier to bear.

- Encourage them to talk to health professionals about how they feel. There may be extra physical and emotional care available that they are unaware of. If they have had an ectopic or molar pregnancy in the past, they should always be given an early scan. Early scans are not routine after one miscarriage, but if they can't access one on the NHS, they may wish to find a private provider. Many midwives are happy to see women who have had a previous loss more often.

- Encourage them to look for other support – for example the Miscarriage Association's Pregnancy After Loss group. Some people find it helpful to talk to others who are going through something similar. Others prefer not to be part of a group where anxieties are spelled out and there is sometimes bad news as well as good. Some people may benefit from therapy to help them cope with the feelings that trying to conceive and being pregnant after a loss can bring up.

- If all goes well, keep in touch after the birth. They may feel anxious and struggle to relax into parenthood. They may suffer from postnatal mental health difficulties, but feel unable to reach out for help. They may worry that people will think they 'should' be blissfully happy now they have what they wanted so much, and there is no room for any difficult emotions. But parenting a newborn is hard for almost everyone. Don't assume they are coping well; ask them how they are doing and be there to listen.

- Don't assume that a successful pregnancy means they have forgotten the baby or babies they lost. Acknowledge and recognize they existed as part of the joy of celebrating a birth.

"Parenting a newborn is hard for almost everyone. Don't assume they are coping well; ask them how they are doing and be there to listen."

"I think I maybe tried to taper both her and my excitement because I was scared of the fallout if it all happened again. We talked about that too, though, and I think we both came to the realization (though I'm not sure I can say I really let myself go) that we had to try to be excited and not let the worry outweigh that."

Keyan

9

LOOKING AFTER YOURSELF

"When I'm feeling run-down or exhausted, I always try to remind myself that you can't pour from an empty cup. It helps me feel OK about taking some time for myself too."
Vic

It's really important to look after yourself while supporting someone else. You need to stay well and make sure you have time to process your own emotions too. There is strength in recognizing and responding to your own needs and, in the long-term, this will be more helpful for everyone involved.

I've spoken a lot in earlier chapters about how you might be affected if you are the partner. In this chapter, there's guidance on how to look after yourself.

As a friend or family member, you may be affected too. You may find it hard to understand or empathize as much as the person you are supporting needs. It can be draining to spend a lot of time trying to work out what to say and do to help. You may really want to make things better for them and feel sad that you can't make their pain go away.

They may be dealing with things in a way that feels very different to how you would, or did. This can be frustrating, especially if their actions are affecting your family or friendship group. On top of this frustration, you may feel guilty for feeling this way at all, or even angry about how things have turned out.

"You may be grieving the loss too – the grief may not be as strong as that felt by the person you are supporting, but it is still important to acknowledge it."

You may feel guilty about your own pregnancy or children, or hurt that someone you were so close to doesn't want to see you right now. You may not be able to help feeling this way, and wish you didn't. Complicated emotions can be exhausting and take time to work through. Or you may feel more worried about your own pregnancy or future pregnancies after seeing what the person you are supporting has been through.

You may be grieving the loss too – as a grandparent or other family member. The grief may not be as strong as that felt by the person you are supporting, but it is still important to acknowledge it. Their loss may bring back memories of your own experiences in the recent or more distant past. Grandparents, in particular, may have been through something similar at a time when it wasn't considered 'appropriate' to talk about it or to mourn. They may find themselves processing emotions relating to their own loss.

The person you are supporting may be very reliant on you for support, which can be exhausting and may mean you have no time for yourself. At the same time, they may take difficult emotions out on you. This can be hurtful, especially when you feel you are doing all you can to help them.

I have divided the suggestions below into those for partners and those for family and friends, but you may find suggestions from both sections helpful.

LOOKING AFTER YOURSELF AS A PARTNER

- Give yourself time to grieve. When you spend a lot of time looking after your partner's needs, your own feelings can become buried. Spend some time working out how you feel about what has happened. You are certainly not alone if you need to process difficult emotions. Research has found that most (but not all) partners feel sadness, grief and shock after a loss, but sometimes these feelings show themselves in different ways.[32] Just because you are not grieving in the same way as your partner, doesn't mean you are not feeling things too. Some partners find that chatting with a therapist, peer supporter or bereavement midwife is more useful than they anticipated.

- Talking tends to help. Talk to your partner of course (see Chapters 4 and 5). Find someone else you trust too. If you have a friend who has been through something similar, make time to message them, chat or meet up. It's up to you who you tell but many partners have found that sharing something of their experience publicly may mean it's easier to start talking about it with friends or family.

"Mates often started the conversation. They were ready to listen. One said how brave he thought we'd both been in being open about our losses. That sparked a long and not entirely sober discussion with four or five male friends over pints. Another friend, a guy from work who had recently been through a miscarriage with his wife, said he'd found a piece of journalism I had written about miscarriage and told me how comforting he had found it to know other men were experiencing similar emotions. There was something almost beautiful about it."
Keyan

- Charity helplines can be a wonderful source of support for you as well as your partner. If you're not sure what to say, tell them so. They can help you find the words. I've included details of helplines, live chat, email and online support communities in Useful Resources.
- You may feel you have to stay strong for your partner, but a lot of people actually find it helpful to see their partner is grieving too. Mourning together may help you both.
- Some workplaces will offer counselling or other support, for example as part of an employee assistance programme or through workplace health insurance. Do seek it out if you feel you need it – it's your right as an employee, so you may as well use it. It's also worth checking if your company has a miscarriage policy in place, as you may be entitled to some leave. If they don't have a policy or an automatic entitlement, it's still worth asking your manager. Workplaces are encouraged to offer bereavement or compassionate leave to partners who need it.
- Even if you genuinely don't feel you are struggling with difficult feelings about the loss, it's important to take care of yourself when you are supporting someone who is. What do you usually do to feel good? Make time for it. Be kind to yourself, especially if you find yourself absorbing difficult emotions from others. Remind yourself that you

are a safe space for the person you are supporting – it's only because they are comfortable with you that they feel able to release their most difficult and ugly feelings.

- Some people find it helpful to read about others' experiences. It can help them feel less alone, understand their own responses and find new ways to cope. The Miscarriage Association publishes a number of filmed and written stories from partners, in the 'partners' section of their website. You can also find these on Instagram and Twitter hashtags – see Useful Resources.

- You may find that research and information can help you feel more in control, especially if you have felt helpless so far. There is a lot of information on websites such as the Miscarriage Association and Tommy's (see Useful Resources). Do be aware there may be no clear answers to why you and your partner experienced this particular loss.

- You may need time to understand and recognize your feelings and space to work through them. Remember, it's OK not to be OK. You may find that particular events and anniversaries bring things back in unexpected ways.

- If your partner is very reliant on you for support, and you are feeling the strain, have a look at the section on helping them access further support (see page 113). You may also find the section on miscarriage and mental health problems useful (see page 33). You do not need to stop being there for your partner, but you may be able to find different sources of help to take some of the pressure off yourself.

LOOKING AFTER YOURSELF AS A FAMILY MEMBER OR FRIEND

"I had conflicting emotions, crying and trying to be strong for my sister. I didn't reach out to anyone for support for myself, as I didn't feel comfortable talking about her and her situation to anyone else. Being open about my own emotions helped. At first I tried to hide my upset as I didn't want to upset her more, but once I told her I cried too, it was clear to see she needed to know and see other people were upset too."

Sarah (supporting her sister who had five miscarriages)

- Some of the information above may help. Charity helplines are there for family and friends too. They will be happy to talk through your feelings about the loss or help you think about how you can help. They are confidential, so you don't need to worry about sharing private experiences with other people.
- It's usually OK to show your own sadness about the loss – or losses – to the person you are supporting. Many people

feel comforted by the idea that they are not alone in their grief. Give yourself time to grieve if the loss has affected you too.

- If they are behaving in a way that you find hurtful or difficult to understand, talk to someone you trust – perhaps your own partner, another friend or someone on a confidential helpline. Remember, we all have different experiences and deal with them in different ways. The person you are supporting is dealing with a tough situation in the best way they know. They are probably feeling very mixed up. Try to be patient and kind, whilst getting support for yourself elsewhere.

- If you are pregnant and finding that offering support is making you very worried or stressed about your own pregnancy, it's OK to take a step back to look after yourself. Talk about your feelings with someone you trust. You might also find it helpful to talk to any healthcare professionals looking after you. You could ask another friend or family member to offer some further support in the meantime.

- As I mention in the partners section above, you should also make time for yourself, especially if you are offering a lot of support. Make a conscious effort to keep doing things that make you feel good.

A LAST THANK YOU

This book was unlikely to have been an easy read. But it was an important one. Thousands of people go through miscarriage, ectopic pregnancy or molar pregnancy without the right support. We need more people like you. People who take these losses seriously. People who have the sensitivity to recognize that they don't know, the commitment to find out more and the courage to say something, however small, with support and love. I hope you find the stories, suggestions and ideas helpful, both for yourself and the people you care about. Please do spread the word.

Thank you.

ACKNOWLEDGEMENTS

Thank you to Ruth Bender Atik, who extremely kindly agreed to write the foreword and, more importantly, has been a wonderful boss and friend over the last eight years. Thanks also to Dr Marjory MacLean, retired obstetrician and Lead for Early Pregnancy who gave me many helpful comments and advice on the more medical chapters. Any mistakes are entirely my own.

Thanks to Dr Petra Boynton, Julia Bueno and Miranda Ward, whose wonderful books (see Useful Resources) helped with my research. Thanks also to Jody Day of Gateway Women, Denise McGuiness from UCD Midwifery, Silvana Tillman, Claire Mitchell, Chloe and Pete and everyone from Sands Utd Huddersfield FC, and the Worst Girl Gang Ever Facebook group.

Thank you to everyone who courageously shared what were often painful and traumatic experiences in order to help others understand. I've included extracts and quotes from some, but every one of them helped shape this book.

Finally, thank you to my husband Alex. Our wedding rings are engraved with the reminder to 'be silly and kind'. His kindness has helped me through the toughest of times and he's still as silly as the day we met.

ENDNOTES

1. *Registering a stillbirth*. www.gov.uk/register-stillbirth
   [Accessed October 2020]
2. Miscarriage Association – *Information on Miscarriage*.
   www.miscarriageassociation.org.uk/information/
   miscarriage [Accessed July 2020]
   Tommy's *Research into Miscarriage*. www.tommys.org/our-
   organisation/our-research/research-miscarriage [Accessed
   July 2020]
   Stray-Pederson B & Stray-Pederson S (1984). 'Etiologic factors
   and subsequent reproductive performance in 195 couples
   with a prior history of habitual abortion.' *American Journal
   of Obstetrics & Gynaecology*. 148: 2: 140-146. Available at
   pubmed.ncbi.nlm.nih.gov/6691389/ [Accessed July 2020]
   Liddell, Pattinson & Zanderigo (1991). 'Recurrent
   miscarriage – outcome after supportive care in early
   pregnancy.' *Australian & New Zealand Journal of
   Obstetrics & Gynaecology*. 1991; 31: 4: 320-322.

Coomarasamy A et al. (2019). The PRISM trial. 'A
Randomized Trial of Progesterone in Women with
Bleeding in Early Pregnancy.' *N Engl J Med.* Available
at www.nejm.org/doi/full/10.1056/NEJMoa1813730
[Accessed July 2020]

Coomarasamy A et al. (2015). 'The PROMISE trial.
Randomised Trial of Progesterone in Women with Recurrent
Miscarriages.' *N Engl J Med.* Available at www.nejm.org/
doi/full/10.1056/NEJMoa150492 [Accessed July 2020]

Brigham, Conlon & Farquharson (1999). 'A longitudinal
study of pregnancy outcome following idiopathic
recurrent miscarriage.' *Human Reproduction*; 14: 11:
2868- 2871.

N Maconochie, P Doyle, S Prior, R Simmons (2007). 'Risk
factors for first trimester miscarriage: results from a UK
population-based case-control study.' *BJOG*; 114(2):170-186.

Sharma R, Agarwal A, Rohra VK, Assidi M, AbuElmagd M,
Turki RF (2015). 'Effects of increased paternal age on sperm
quality, reproductive outcome and associated epigenetic
risks to offspring.' *Reprod Biol Endocrinol*; 13: 35.

Boots C, Stephenson MD (2011). 'Does obesity increase
the risk of miscarriage in spontaneous conception? A
systematic review.' *Semin Reprod Med*; 29(6): 507-13.

Bonde JP1, Jørgensen KT, Bonzini M, Palmer KT (2013).
'Miscarriage and occupational activity: a systematic

review and meta-analysis regarding shift work, working hours, lifting, standing, and physical workload.' *Scand J Work Environ Health*; 39(4): 325-34.

3. Miscarriage Association Leaflet – *Why Me?* www.miscarriageassociation.org.uk/leaflet/why-me [Accessed August 2020]

4. Miscarriage Association Leaflet – *Ectopic Pregnancy* www.miscarriageassociation.org.uk/wpcontent/ uploads/2016/10/Ectopic-pregnancy.pdf [Accessed August 2020]

5. National Institute for Health and Care Excellence (2012). NICE clinical guideline (CG154) 'Ectopic pregnancy and miscarriage: Diagnosis and initial management in early pregnancy of ectopic pregnancy and miscarriage.' Available at www.nice.org.uk/guidance/ CG154 [Accessed August 2020]

6. The Ectopic Pregnancy Trust – *Trying to Conceive.* ectopic.org.uk/patients/trying-to-conceive [Accessed July 2020]

7. The Ectopic Pregnancy Trust – *Reasons for an Ectopic Pregnancy.* ectopic.org.uk/patients/reasons-for-an-ectopic-pregnancy [Accessed July 2020]

8. NHS.uk Molar pregnancy information. www.nhs.uk/ conditions/molar-pregnancy [Accessed July 2020] My Molar Pregnancy Information. mymolarpregnancy.

com/information [Accessed August 2020]

9. Farren, Jalmbrant, Ameye et al (2016). 'Post-traumatic stress, anxiety and depression following miscarriage or ectopic pregnancy: a prospective cohort study.' Available at bmjopen.bmj.com/content/6/11/e011864 [Accessed October 2020]

Lok IH, Yip AS, Lee DT, et al (2008). 'A 1-year longitudinal study of psychological morbidity after miscarriage.' *Fertil Steril* 2010;93: 1966–75. doi:10.1016/j.fertnstert.2008.12.048

Toffola, Koponen, Partonen (2013). 'Miscarriage and mental health: Results of two population-based studies' Available at doi.org/10.1016/j.psychres.2012.08.029 [Accessed October 2020]

Van den Akker (2011). 'The psychological and social consequences of miscarriage.' *Expert Rev Obstet. Gynecol* 6(3). Available at www.tandfonline.com/doi/full/10.1586/eog.11.14 [Accessed October 2020]

Annsofie Adolfsson (2011). 'Meta-analysis to obtain a scale of psychological reaction after perinatal loss: focus on miscarriage' *Psychology Research and Behaviour Management* 2011:4 29–39

10. Mind.org.uk *Information and support.* www.mind.org.uk/information-support [Accessed August 2020]

11. Armstrong, D (2001). 'Exploring Fathers' Experiences of

Pregnancy After a Prior Perinatal Loss', MCN: *The American Journal of Maternal/Child Nursing*. Available at www.journals.lww.com/mcnjournal/Fulltext/2001/05000/Exploring_Fathers__Experiences_of_Pregnancy_After.12.aspx [Accessed September 2020]

12. The Miscarriage Association – *Counselling After a Miscarriage*. www.miscarriageassociation.org.uk/your-feelings/counselling-after-a-miscarriage [Accessed August 2020]

13. National Institute for Health and Care Excellence Clinical Guidance [CG192] (Dec 2014, Updated Feb 2020). Available at www.nice.org.uk/guidance/cg192/chapter/1-Recommendations [Accessed September 2020] National Institute for Health and Care Excellence. Clinical Knowledge Summaries. Pregnant woman on an antidepressant (July 2020) Available at cks.nice.org.uk/topics/depression-antenatal-postnatal/management/pregnant-on-an-antidepressant [Accessed August 2020]

14. North Bristol Trust NHS – *Antidepressant Use During Pregnancy*. Available at www.nbt.nhs.uk/maternity-services/pregnancy/antidepressant-use-during-pregnancy [Accessed Sept 2020]

15. NHS.uk *Study Probes Stress and Conception* (2010). Available at www.nhs.uk/news/pregnancy-and-child/study-probes-stress-and-conception/#:~:text=The%20researchers%20concluded%20that%20

%E2%80%9Cstress,when%20attempting%20to%20
achieve%20pregnancy%E2%80%9D [Accessed Sept 2020]

16. Samaritans – *Myths About Suicide*. Available at www.
samaritans.org/how-we-can-help/if-youre-worried-about-
someone-else/myths-about-suicide [Accessed Sept 2020]

17. Mind – *Supporting Someone Who Feels Suicidal, About
Suicidal Feelings* (2020). Available at www.mind.org.uk/
information-support/helping-someone-else/supporting-
someone-who-feels-suicidal/about-suicidal-feelings
[Accessed August 2020]

18. Miscarriage Association – *Information and
Support for Employees* (2020). Available at www.
miscarriageassociation.org.uk/information/miscarriage-
and-the-workplace/employees-information-and-support
[Accessed September 2020]

19. Ibid.

20. Gateway Women. Available at gateway-women.com
[Accessed August 2020]

21. The Miscarriage Association – *When the Trying Stops*.
Available at www.miscarriageassociation.org.uk/wp-
content/uploads/2016/10/When-the-Trying-Stops.pdf
[Accessed Sept 2020]

22. Kangatharan C, Labram S, Bhattacharya S (2016).
'Interpregnancy interval following miscarriage and
adverse pregnancy outcomes: systematic review and

meta-analysis' *Human Reproduction Update* 23; 2, March-April 2017; 221–231. Available at doi.org/10.1093/humupd/dmw043 [Accessed October 2020]

23. The Miscarriage Association – *Thinking About Another Pregnancy*. Available at www.miscarriageassociation.org.uk/wp-content/uploads/2016/10/Thinking-about-another-pregnancy.pdf [Accessed September 2020]

24. *Coping with Pregnancy Loss*. Available at copingwithpregnancyloss.com [Accessed September 2020]

25. The Miscarriage Association – *When the Trying Stops*. Available at www.miscarriageassociation.org.uk/wp-content/uploads/2016/10/When-the-Trying-Stops.pdf [Accessed Sept 2020]

26. Fertility network – *Life Without Children*. Available at fertilitynetworkuk.org/life-without-children [Accessed October 2020]

27. Baby loss awareness. Available at babyloss-awareness.org [Accessed October 2020]

28. The Miscarriage Association virtual hugs campaign. Available at www.miscarriageassociation.org.uk/your-feelings/supporting-someone-through-pregnancy-loss/virtualhugs [Accessed October 2020]
The Miscarriage Association pregnancy loss cards. Available at www.miscarriageassociation.org.uk/product-

category/pregnancy-loss-cards [Accessed October 2020]

29. The Miscarriage Association – *Marking Your Loss*.
Available at www.miscarriageassociation.org.uk/your-
feelings/marking-your-loss [Accessed October 2020]

30. The Miscarriage Association – *How We Help*. Online
Support. Available at www.miscarriageassociation.org.uk/
how-we-help/online-support [Accessed October 2020]

31. Stray-Pedersen B, Stray-Pedersen S (1984). 'Etiologic
factors and subsequent reproductive performance in 195
couples with a prior history of habitual abortion.' *Am
J Obstet Gynecol*. Jan 15;148(2): 140-6. doi: 10.1016/
s0002-9378(84)80164-7. PMID: 6691389.
Liddell HS, Pattison NS, Zanderigo A (1991). 'Recurrent
miscarriage – outcome after supportive care in early
pregnancy' *Aust N Z J Obstet Gynaecol*. Nov;31(4):
320-2. doi: 10.1111/j.1479-828x.1991.tb02811.x. PMID:
1799343.

32. Boynton P (2014). 'Research into partners feelings after
a loss.' University College London. More information
available at www.ucl.ac.uk/news/2014/jul/partners-
miscarriage-sufferers-ignored [Accessed October 2020]

USEFUL RESOURCES

PREGNANCY LOSS

Babyloss International Support (a list of international pregnancy loss support resources): www.babyloss.com

UK

- Baby Loss Awareness Week: www.babyloss-awareness.org
- The Ectopic Pregnancy Trust: www.ectopic.org.uk
- Miscarriage Association: www.miscarriageassociation.org.uk
- The Mix (support for under 25s): www.themix.org.uk
- Molar Pregnancy Support and Information: www.molarpregnancy.co.uk
- SANDS (Stillbirth and Neonatal Death Support): www.sands.org.uk

- Saying Goodbye: www.sayinggoodbye.org
- Tommy's: www.tommys.org
- Twin's Trust Bereavement Support Group: www.twinstrust.org/bereavement

USA

- Babies Remembered: wintergreenpress.org
- CLIMB (Center for Loss in Multiple Birth): www.climb-support.org
- International Stillbirth Alliance: www.stillbirthalliance.org
- March of Dimes: www.marchofdimes.org
- MISS Foundation: missfoundation.org
- My Molar Pregnancy: www.mymolarpregnancy.com
- Remembering Our Babies: www.october15th.com
- SHARE: www.nationalshareoffice.com

Australia and New Zealand

- Gidget Foundation: gidgetfoundation.org.au
- Miscarriage Support: www.miscarriagesupport.org.nz
- Miscarriage, Stillbirth and Newborn Death Support: www.sands.org.au
- Pink Elephants: www.pinkelephants.org.au

FERTILITY AND INFERTILITY

- Gateway Women: www.gateway-women.com
- UK: Fertility Network UK: www.fertilitynetworkuk.org
- USA: RESOLVE: resolve.org
- Australia: Fertility Support Australia: fertilitysupport.org.au

MEDICATION IN PREGNANCY

- Wrisk (understanding and improving the communication of risk relating to pregnancy): www.wrisk.org
- Choice and Medication: www.choiceandmedication.org
- Bumps (best use of medicines in pregnancy): www.medicinesinpregnancy.org/Medicine--pregnancy

EMPLOYMENT SUPPORT

- UK: ACAS: www.acas.org.uk
- UK: Citizens Advice: www.citizensadvice.org.uk
- UK: Amy McKeown, who shares her story in this book, is campaigning to create clear legal definitions and a defined legal construct of 'pregnancy-related illness': support the campaign at amymckeown.com/campaign

- USA: Labor Laws and Issues: www.usa.gov/labor-laws
- Australia: www.fairwork.gov.au
- New Zealand: www.employment.govt.nz

RELATIONSHIP SUPPORT

- UK: Relate: www.relate.org.uk
- USA: Love is respect: www.loveisrespect.org
- Australia: Relationships Australia: www.relationships.org.au
- Sexual Advice Association: www.sexualadviceassociation.co.uk

MEMORIAL JEWELLERY

- There are many options on sites such as Etsy, all offering something unique:
  www.etsy.com/uk/market/memorial_jewelry
- Lisa Matthews Jewellery: www.lisamatthewsjewellery.co.uk

REMOVING TARGET ADVERTISING

- A digital bereavement checklist: www.wishfulinkingpress.com/digital-bereavement-checklist
- Removing ads from Facebook: offspring.lifehacker.com/how-to-remove-pregnancy-and-baby-ads-from-your-facebook-1824285483
- In the UK you can make a complaint to the Information Commissioner if you are not unsubscribed as requested: ico.org.uk/make-a-complaint/nuisance-calls-and-messages/spam-emails/report-spam-emails

FACEBOOK SUPPORT GROUPS

- Tommy's Baby Loss Support Group: www.facebook.com/groups/Tommysblsupport
- The Miscarriage Association Pregnancy After Loss Private Group: www.facebook.com/groups/miscarriageassociationpregnantafterloss
- The Miscarriage Association Private Group: www.facebook.com/groups/208106969238866/about
- The Miscarriage Association Public Group: www.facebook.com/groups/8033009179/about

- The Worst Girl Gang Ever – Miscarriage and Pregnancy Loss Support Group: www.facebook.com/groups/261891265038126/about
- My Molar Pregnancy Support Group: www.facebook.com/groups/mymolarpregnancy
- Ectopic Pregnancy Support Group: www.facebook.com/groups/275366965831264

TWITTER CHATS

#BabyLossHour: Tuesdays at 8pm (GMT)
#childlesshour: Sundays at 8pm (GMT)

HASHTAGS

These are just a few examples. Search on your chosen platform to find and connect to others. Most people use lowercase but capitalizing each new word helps people with screen readers.
#babyloss
#BabyLossAwarenessWeek
#ectopicpregnancy
#lateloss
#LGBTBabyLoss
#miscarriage
#pregnancyloss

BOOKS

Boynton, Petra, *Coping with Pregnancy Loss*, Routledge (2018)

Bueno, Julia, *The Brink of Being*, Virago Press (2019)

Day, Jody, *Living the Life Unexpected*, Bluebird (2020)

Hepburn, Jessica, *The Pursuit of Motherhood*, Matador (2014)

Ward, Miranda, *Adrift: Fieldnotes from Almost-Motherhood*, W&N (2021)

GENERAL MENTAL HEALTH SUPPORT

UK

- Anxiety UK: www.anxietyuk.org.uk
- Heads Together: www.headstogether.org.uk
- Hub of Hope: hubofhope.co.uk
- Mental Health Foundation UK: www.mentalhealth.org.uk
- Mind UK: www.mind.org.uk
- MindWise: www.mindwisenv.org
- Rethink Mental Illness: www.rethink.org
- Samaritans: www.samaritans.org, helpline: 116 123
- Scottish Association for Mental Health (SAMH) (Scotland): www.samh.org.uk
- Shout: www.giveusashout.org, text 85258
- Young Minds: www.youngminds.org.uk

USA

- Anxiety & Depression Association of America: adaa.org
- HelpGuide: www.helpguide.org
- Mentalhealth.gov: www.mentalhealth.gov
- Mental Health America: www.mhanational.org
- National Alliance on Mental Illness (NAMI): www.nami.org
- National Institute of Mental Health: www.nimh.nih.gov
- Very Well Mind: www.verywellmind.com

Australia and New Zealand

- Anxiety New Zealand Trust: www.anxiety.org.nz
- Beyond Blue: www.beyondblue.org.au
- Head to Health: headtohealth.gov.au
- Health Direct: www.healthdirect.gov.au
- Mental Health Australia: mhaustralia.org
- Mental Health Foundation of New Zealand: www.mentalhealth.org.nz
- SANE Australia: www.sane.org

TriggerHub.org is one of the most elite and scientifically proven forms of mental health intervention

Trigger Publishing is the leading independent mental health and wellbeing publisher in the UK and US. Clinical and scientific research conducted by assistant professor Dr Kristin Kosyluk and her highly acclaimed team in the Department of Mental Health Law & Policy at the University of South Florida (USF), as well as complementary research by her peers across the US, has independently verified the power of lived experience as a core component in achieving mental health prosperity. Specifically, the lived experiences contained within our bibliotherapeutic books are intrinsic elements in reducing stigma, making those with poor mental health feel less alone, providing the privacy they need to heal, ensuring they know the essential steps to kick-start their own journeys to recovery, and providing hope and inspiration when they need it most.

Delivered through TriggerHub, our unique online portal and accompanying smartphone app, we make our library of bibliotherapeutic titles and other vital resources accessible to individuals and organizations anywhere, at any time and with complete privacy, a crucial element of recovery. As such, TriggerHub is the primary recommendation across the UK and US for the delivery of lived experiences.

At Trigger Publishing and TriggerHub, we proudly lead the way in making the unseen become seen. We are dedicated to humanizing mental health, breaking stigma and challenging outdated societal values to create real action and impact. Find out more about our world-leading work with lived experience and bibliotherapy via triggerhub. org, or by joining us on:

🐦 @triggerhub_

ⓕ @triggerhub.org

📷 @triggerhub_

Printed in the USA
CPSIA information can be obtained
at www.ICGtesting.com
JSHW031713140824
68134JS00038B/3674

9 781837 962549